P9-DCR-665

Contents

YOUR NEIGHBOR'S FAITH

A Lutheran Looks at Other Churches

YOUR NEIGHBOR'S FAITH

BY W. A. POOVEY

OMNIA VINCIT VERITAS

THY WORD IS TRUTH

Augsburg Publishing House · Minneapolis

YOUR NEIGHBOR'S FAITH

Copyright © 1959, 1960 and 1961 Augsburg Publishing House

Library of Congress Catalog Card No. 61-6998

Fourth Printing, December 1961

A reprint of articles that appeared in ONE
magazine from May 1959 to November 1960.

MANUFACTURED IN THE UNITED STATES OF AMERICA

Preface

The chapters in this booklet first appeared as a series in ONE, Lutheran youth monthly, during 1959 and 1960. ONE presented the series of 17 articles in answer to a perpetual request from youth for comparative information on other denominations. Readers of ONE said they wanted such information briefly, non-technically, and in a way that would show similarities and differences between Lutheranism and the other Christian families.

To perform the daring task of squeezing each denomination's story into a few typewritten pages, we called on W. A. Poovey, who teaches the art of preaching at Wartburg Seminary, Dubuque, Iowa. If ability to organize complex material and to say much in few words are needed for good preaching, then Prof. Poovey is teaching the right subject. For helpful organization and well-chosen words characterize his articles.

A few qualifications should be kept in mind as you read the following chapters:

1. They are written from a Lutheran point of view. This material does not pretend to be objective or unbiased. Each chapter is a comparative study which says, "Here is how this group looks to a Lutheran." At the same time, the material seeks to be fair, to reflect the other churches as they themselves teach and practice. It grants others the right to hold their opinions and discusses differences which do exist, without dwelling on differences which are minor or imagined.

2. They are written in a popular vein. These comparisons are brief and non-technical, often using colloquial language. They are not doctrinal studies of the sort theologians write for theologians, though they do deal with doctrines. They seek to offer over-all impressions rather than precise, scholarly definitions. Thus, the reader who is interested as a student of any group is urged to go beyond these comparisons into the more complete, more technical, and more formal studies which are available.

3. They are written about groups having Christian origins. Some of the chapters deal with religious groups which are not always considered a part of the Church of Christ as traditionally defined. There are those who believe that such groups as the Mormons, the Jehovah's Witnesses, the Christian Scientists, and the Unitarian-Universalists have separated themselves from the mainstream of Christianity and now occupy, at best, a fringe position. These groups are included here because they have grown out of Christian origins, and more or less claim to be a part of the Christian tradition. But other religious groups, which have no Christian origin, such as Judaism or the Baha'i faith, are not included.

The chapters include 15 looks at individual churches or families (e.g., the Baptist family, the Eastern Orthodox family). In addition, there is a concluding chapter which gives a glimpse of 10 smaller but significant groups, and an introduction which offers an overview of our denominational crazy-quilt. Membership figures are generally for the United States alone and are as of the beginning of 1960; they come from the 1961 *Yearbook of American Churches* published by the National Council of the Churches of Christ.

It is hoped that your understanding of your Christian neighbor's faith will grow through use of this booklet.

CHARLES LUTZ
Editor of ONE

Contents

Chapter One

A Crazy-Quilt of Denominations

INTRODUCTION

A few years ago a popular song proclaimed: "They've got an awful lot of coffee in Brazil." Someone could have written a parody with the words: "They've got an awful lot of churches in America." For the United States has more different types of churches within its borders than any other nation in the world. We boast or perhaps shamefully admit to 300 varieties of religious groups.

If you live in a small community, you probably have four or five denominations represented. If the town is medium-sized, it's not unusual for the list of churches to include 10 to 15 groups. In a large city, the church page may carry such strange names as the Christadelphians, the Reorganized Church of Jesus Christ of Latter-Day Saints, or the Fire-Baptized Holiness Church of God of the Americas.

Usually this denominational patchwork quilt doesn't bother most of us. We believe in "live and let live" as far as religion is concerned. But we become disturbed when our social contacts are disrupted by divisions in the church. You may find that your best friend in school is a Methodist and has very strange opinions about your Lutheran Church. Or perhaps you get interested in a girl friend and then are warned away because "she's a Roman Catholic." You note that the crowd at school and the crowd at Luther League isn't the same, because so many school friends are members of youth groups in their own churches.

Of course the greatest problem with denominations isn't the social disruptions that are produced. Our contacts with others simply make us *aware* that the church in America is split into all kinds of segments. We can't help wondering, "How did this happen? What do these other churches teach? How seriously do they differ from the Lutheran Church?"

These are good questions to ask and to answer. Most of us are going to live all our life in a land where the church is divided and therefore we need to be informed about these differences. If we don't know something about denominations, we may be unfair to others. Did you ever hear anyone say, "The Lutheran Church is just like the Roman Catholic"? Or, "Lutherans are all Germans"? Such misguided notions make us angry, but it's possible that we have equally prejudiced notions about others. We need to know in order to be fair.

Moreover, almost everyone gets the feeling at times that the grass is greener on the other side of the fence. We may think the Baptists have a better church program than our own, or we may be attracted by the air of awe and mystery that surrounds Roman Catholic worship. I once knew a

Lutheran woman who told the organist at a Methodist church how much she liked Methodist hymns. To her astonishment, the organist lamented that her church didn't have the beautiful hymns we sing in the Lutheran service.

So it goes. We need to know the differences among churches in order to know our own values. So in these articles we'll be viewing the major religious groupings in America, their teachings, their worship and life, and the points where they agree and disagree with the Lutheran church.

But now let's take a broad look at the denominational crazy-quilt that is America. Why *do* we have so many different groups here? What produces denominations anyway? Why should there be more than one church when there is only one Lord and Savior? The following three truths will help us to gain an insight into the puzzle of a divided church.

1. *Denominations are not something new in the Christian Church.* Most Lutherans know that Martin Luther was the first of the great reformers, at least the first to make an open break with the teachings of medieval Roman Catholicism. Sometimes this fact gives us a sense of guilt. We wonder whether our church must bear the responsibility for the divided state of Christianity. We may be tempted to think that it might have been better to have accepted the abuses and preserved the unity of the church.

What we need to remember is that in this imperfect world denominations are almost inevitable. The Christian church did not remain truly united for long, and its seeming unity at Luther's time was a sham.

As a matter of fact, the first evidences of a divided church appeared in New Testament times. Paul, writing to the Christians at Corinth, noted that there was dissension in the church and then he defined the trouble: "What I mean is that each one of you says, 'I belong to Paul,' or 'I belong to Apollos,' or 'I belong to Cephas,' or 'I belong to Christ'" (I Cor. 1:12). While this division was apparently healed, it reflected the almost inevitable temptation for Christians to unite around popular leaders and to quarrel with other Christians.

Did you ever hear of the Gnostics, the Ebionites, the Marcionites, the Donatists? Unless you're an A-plus student in church history, these names are very strange to you. Yet all these groups existed in the early centuries of the Christian era. Each one was a denomination, a group that disagreed in some ways with other believers.

Most of us have the idea, however, that somehow the church was united for a long period of time—until the Reformation. In a sense that's true, but when we know how it was done it doesn't seem so remarkable or praiseworthy. Suppose our Congress would pass a law that every American must belong to the Presbyterian Church. Suppose the whole power of the government could be exerted to enforce such a law by charging all dissenters with heresy and treason. If the police power were strong enough and it managed to execute enough people, we might have a unified church in America.

That's precisely what happened during a long period of human history. The church and the state in Western Europe combined to enforce uniformity. The natural tendency for people to disagree on religious matters was checked, but at what a cost! Even with all the power of church and state united against them, such independent groups as the Waldensians in Italy, the Hussites in Bohemia and the Lollards in England managed to spring up and become separate denominations.

Thus, regrettable though it may be, the tendency to form separate groups in the Christian church seems an inevitable one. It cannot be laid at the door of Luther or any other individual. Sometimes it reflects the perversity of individuals. Sometimes it is the result of unwillingness on the part of the existing church to preach the pure Gospel. A separate denomination may become the Lord's means of accomplishing His work.

2. *Denominations are inevitable in America.* We like to brag about our bigness in America. Is our divided church one more evidence that we have more of everything, including denominations, than other people? Not quite. Two things must be remembered.

First, we have permitted religious freedom in the United States longer than any other major nation in the world. Lord James Bryce, a titled Englishman, wrote a famous book called *The American Commonwealth.* In it he said: "Of all the differences between the Old World and the New, this is perhaps the most salient. . . . All religious bodies are absolutely equal before the law and unrecognized by law, except as voluntary associations of private citizens." Such freedom in America naturally allowed denominations to grow and to divide into other groups.

Suppose you decided that you wanted to start a church of your own. You have perfect freedom in America to do so. You could buy land for a church building. You could ring doorbells and invite people to attend your services.

You could print and distribute literature without any interference. Such liberty was not found in most lands until recent years and is still not enjoyed by millions of people. Thus America has offered opportunities for the development of denominations unrivalled anywhere.

Secondly, we have managed to import religous groups from every part of the globe. Many of the early settlers, including Lutherans, came to the New World seeking religious liberty. Later it was poverty and the hope of a new life that brought people here. Emma Lazarus' famous inscription for the Statue of Liberty reflects that movement:

> *Give me your tired, your poor,*
> *Your huddled masses yearning to breathe free,*
> *The wretched refuse of your teeming shore,*
> *Send these, the homeless, tempest-tossed, to me:*
> *I lift my lamp beside the golden door.*

At the peak of the immigration movement, more than a million people from Europe and Asia entered this country in a single year—1907! Quite obviously these people brought their religions with them. Each group added to the quantity of denominations here.

Someone has said that the only really *new* religions that have come into existence in America are the Christian Scientists and the Mormons. All the rest have been imported in one form or another. While that may be a narrow view, the fact remains that American diversity in religion is no greater than would be expected when one considers the way this country was settled.

3. *Don't pay too much attention to the label.* Did you ever listen to a preacher from another denomination and

say to yourself: "He sounds like a Lutheran preacher. That's the way our pastor preaches the Gospel"? You may have been right in such a verdict. For something has happened to many churches in America. Over the course of several centuries they have lost their distinctive features and have grouped themselves around different and broader classifications.

Ask yourself, "What's the difference between a Democrat and a Republican?" Once this was a simple matter to define, in terms of the tariff or other major issues. Today such a definition is almost impossible because there are people in both parties that think alike. There are liberals and conservatives in both groups. Every now and then someone calls for a realignment of the parties but nothing seems to happen.

This same kind of intermingling has occurred in many churches. During the past century some men in many of the denominations have become known as "liberals." Their outlook toward the Bible and the place of the church in the world has been deeply affected by modern science and political action. Thus men in different denominations have found common interests that cut across denominational lines.

As a reaction to the "liberals," there has come to exist in most churches a bloc of pastors and laymen known as "fundamentalists." Sometimes the fundamentalists withdraw into new groups; sometimes they struggle with the liberals for control of a denomination. But they find their allies in most large groups, regardless of denominational leanings.

And standing in the middle in the church has been a group called the conservatives, who do not find the com-

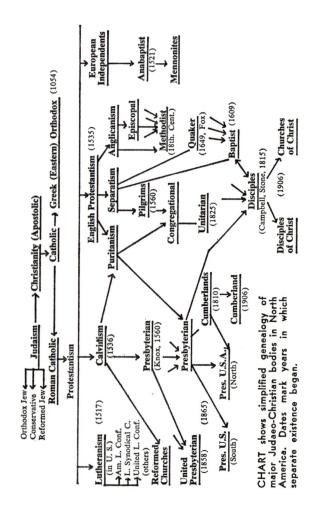

CHART shows simplified genealogy of major Judaeo-Christian bodies in North America. Dates mark years in which separate existence began.

plete answer in either of the extreme groups. Probably our Lutheran churches would best fit into this category and we usually feel kinship with conservative Christians in other groups.

Thus, as someone has said: "There are a lot of Lutherans outside the Lutheran church." (And on the other hand, there are members of Lutheran churches who aren't Lutherans in what they believe.) Labels have lost much of their meaning among Protestantism in general. It's no longer safe to conclude that all Methodists believe in emotional revivals, that all Presbyterians teach predestination, that every Baptist church insists on baptism by immersion.

As a matter of fact, the divisions in the church aren't as great as we sometimes imagine. Three hundred denominations sounds like a terrible situation, but actually about 95% of all Christians in America belong to 10 denominational families. When you consider the lines of interest that cut across denominational barriers, the patchwork quilt of denominations isn't quite as bad as it seems.

Of course, no one likes the thought of a divided church. But since we have all these groups in America, we can at least try to understand their history and their teachings. We'll begin by considering . . . *The Roman Catholics.*

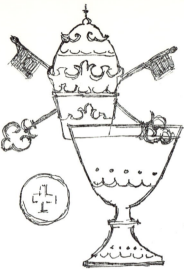

Chapter Two

A Puzzling Mixture

THE ROMAN CATHOLICS

The beautiful music dies away in the great cathedral. From somewhere a bell tinkles mysteriously. The priest lifts a golden chalice toward heaven while the worshipers kneel and reverently cross themselves.

A group of friends meet together for lunch on Friday. They are all the same age and share common interests. But one cannot eat the same food as the others.

An old man is carried on a golden throne through the streets of Rome. He extends his hands in blessing and thousands bow in reverence before him. They greet him with cries of "Evviva il papa."

A young couple want to get married. They are not members of the same church. The bride-to-be insists that the other must sign a contract saying the children of the marriage must be brought up in her church. Otherwise there will be no wedding.

Everyone will recognize these glimpses of Roman Catholicism. However, although the Church of Rome is the largest single denomination in America, and although the first Catholic parish in the present bounds of the United States was established in 1565 at St. Augustine, Florida, most Protestants know little about the Roman Church. And what they know is generally wrong.

It isn't possible in one or even in 10 articles to discuss all the phases of Roman Catholic history and doctrine. But one thought may help explain much that puzzles us. The Roman Church has existed for many centuries, though its claim to be the "original" Christian church is disputed by every rival Christian group. Over the course of many years, the Roman Church has come to terms with the world in many ways. Seemingly rigid, it has yielded on many fronts and now represents Christianity as modified by many of the ideas of men. As someone wittily said: "All men are born Roman Catholics. You have to teach them to become Protestants." Let's see how this works.

1. *Authority*. One of our commonest notions is the idea that men want to be free. Yet this is not always the case. There's something appealing to many people about putting all their trust in a central, all-powerful authority. If we can say, "My father told me to do it," we can shift all blame when anything goes wrong. Herein lies an explanation for the millions who cried: "Heil Hitler," or for those who blindly obeyed Joseph Stalin. Men derive a certain satisfaction if they can escape responsibility.

Roman Catholicism satisfies this desire for many. A certain firm which investigates business methods once reported that the Catholic Church is the most efficiently run business in America. Power is concentrated in the hands of a few and the majority are relieved of responsibility to act or think for themselves.

```
┌─────────────────────────────────────────────┐
│                 STATISTICS                    │
│  Membership .......................... 41,000,000 │
│  Congregations ......................     23,000 │
│  Clergy ...........................     54,000 │
└─────────────────────────────────────────────┘
```

TABLE OF COMPARISON

ROMAN CATHOLICS   LUTHERANS

TEACHINGS

ROMAN CATHOLICS	LUTHERANS
1. Believe in Triune God.	1. Same.
2. Believe in full divinity and full humanity of Christ.	2. Same.
3. Accept the Bible, tradition, and human reason as authority. The Church defines the truth.	3. Accept the Bible alone as authority; the Holy Spirit guides man in interpreting it.
4. Celebrate seven sacraments: baptism, confirmation, penance, communion, marriage, ordination, extreme unction.	4. Celebrate two sacraments: baptism and communion.
5. Believe in Transubstantiation, that is, the bread and wine in communion are magically changed into body and blood of Christ.	5. Believe in Real Presence, that is, communicant receives bread and wine but also the body and blood of Christ.

TYPE OF WORSHIP

ROMAN CATHOLICS	LUTHERANS
Highly liturgical, usually in Latin.	Liturgical but simpler. Same basic form, minus unbiblical additions. In people's language.

GOVERNMENT

ROMAN CATHOLICS	LUTHERANS
An episcopal or hierarchical system with pope as supreme head.	No type of government prescribed. In America, congregational.

PRACTICES

ROMAN CATHOLICS	LUTHERANS
1. Communion to laity in one kind only—the wafer.	1. Communion in both kinds, bread and wine, to clergy and laity.
2. Clergy forbidden to marry.	2. Clergy permitted to marry.
3. Private confession obligatory.	3. Private confession encouraged for those desiring spiritual help.

The chain of authority runs from layman, through parish priest to bishop, cardinal and finally to the pope. Though scriptural evidence is claimed, granting power to the pope as the successor to St. Peter and thus the Vicar of Christ, in reality the pope represents the same concentration of power to be found in any autocratic government or business.

The same principle of authority is demonstrated in the approach to the Bible. When we Protestants read our Bible, we must search for the meaning of God's Word. We must weigh every phrase, compare the different facets of truth and occasionally admit that we can't solve the problem before us. There are times when we wish someone would settle the issues authoritatively, even though we know that's not the way to approach the Bible.

The Roman Catholic has no such difficulty. Contrary to popular report, the Roman Church today *does* encourage Bible reading. But there is no problem of interpretation because the church will settle every issue that arises. If necessary, the pope can speak infallibly and thus solve any dispute. There can be no appeal from such a decision.

That such an authoritative action can lead to teachings at variance with the Bible doesn't seem to disturb. Roman Catholicism recognizes *three* sources of truth—the Bible, tradition and human reason. In juggling these three sources, some queer results are achieved. Thus the idea that Mary was born sinless seems completely contradicted by Scripture, but the other sources provide it.

Because of this different approach to the Bible, Lutherans and Roman Catholics have a difficult time discussing religion. It's like trying to play a football game with each team in a different stadium.

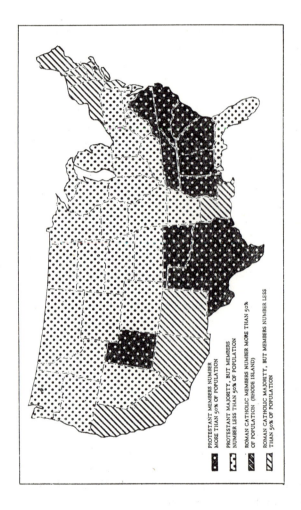

2. *Earning salvation.* If your father offered you a new car, would you refuse it and insist on paying for it? That wouldn't be very smart, but in the area of religion men have always sought to play a part in their own salvation. Though Jesus offers us forgiveness and blessings without any merit on our part, many men find grace hard to accept. Thus the Christians at Galatia relapsed into work-righteousness and had to be warned by Paul against their foolish practices. Even today believers must constantly guard against the idea of earning something in God's sight.

Once again Roman Catholic teachings found a compromise. Catholics believe in the reality of sin just as we do. They also believe in the necessity of Christ's atonement. Therefore we have always considered the Roman Church a Christian group. But they have found a way to satisfy man's desire to try and save himself. So man is encouraged to try to atone for his *actual* sins while Christ takes away the taint of *original* sin.

A whole elaborate system has grown up to satisfy the idea of earning your way to heaven. Thus there are church rules and regulations that make people feel virtuous. Refraining from eating meat on holy days, saying many prayers, attending mass, making pilgrimages—all serve to make satisfaction for sins.

In addition, penance assigned at confession serves the same purpose. The Catholic who confesses a sin is given something to do to wipe out the sting of that sin. And there are saints, including the Virgin Mary, who may be asked for help in such endeavors. Finally even the idea of suffering for a time after death offers a chance to earn a little merit in God's sight.

Most Protestants find the idea of purgatory a terrible one. Yet if a man is bent on earning his own salvation, even the prospect of burning for a while before entering heaven can serve that purpose. We may scorn the compromise between grace and work-righteousness, but it is easy to see how it developed.

3. *The miraculous.* If you want to get a crowd, announce a miracle and thousands will flock to see it. The drawing power of the modern faith-healers is proof of that truth. We are all impressed by something that we cannot explain or understand. In a superstitious world, the appeal of the miraculous is strong.

Once again the Roman Church found a way to satisfy this longing. The simple and beautiful service of Holy Communion, which does contain mysterious elements, was turned into a miracle performed by the priest. According to Roman teaching, the priest possesses the power to change the bread and wine of communion into the actual physical body and blood of Christ. Thus a miracle takes place in the church every time a mass is read. The magically produced body and blood of Christ are then offered to God for the sins of men as an "unbloody repetition of Calvary." Sometimes the members of the church then receive communion, sometimes they don't. It makes no difference, for the really important thing is the miracle of the mass.

Other forms of the miraculous are also found in the church. Thus there are shrines where people can go and be mysteriously healed. The great shrine at Lourdes, France, is the most famous, but there are many others. There are saints who mysteriously bear the *stigmata,* marks on the body similar to the wounds of Christ. There are medals that ward off danger, relics that possess special power, etc. Man's love of the miraculous has found a place in the Roman Church.

4. *Rites and ceremonies.* Human beings love to dress up and parade around. We love parades and fancy spectacles. Schools equip bands with fancy uniforms and the bands go through elaborate gyrations. Lodges flourish on man's love of ritual and ceremony. That such performances often fail to express the real feelings of the participants doesn't disturb us. A parade can stir our hearts even though it is only for a moment.

Christianity as such doesn't possess or demand elaborate ritual. The stress in the Bible is on the changed heart, not on the outward show. Baptism and Holy Communion are simple things in themselves. Preaching and singing seem rather tame to those who want a good show with their religion.

Here again Roman Catholicism found a solution. Over the course of centuries, worship became more and more elaborate to please man's love of show. Today the so-called High Mass, a service with music, is a strange and moving thing. The chanting in Latin, which seems odd to our ears, lends pomp to the service, just as the nonsense cheers at a football game stir up the crowd. The gorgeous robes, the incense, the holy water—all serve to create a mood and stir the worshiper for a moment. Inevitably the preaching of the Word and the real stress on the human heart get neglected in this ritual.

There are other places where elaborate ceremony is performed. The Roman Church celebrates seven sacraments, most of them with much ritual. Thus a young girl once told me that while she was not a Catholic she wanted to get married in a Catholic church because the marriage ceremony was so impressive!

In addition to Baptism, Holy Communion and Marriage, Ordination and Confirmation are both sacraments celebrated with much pomp. Penance is considered a sacrament, though it involves no special ceremony today. Finally there is Extreme Unction, in which Catholics are anointed just before they are about to die. There are other special services too, such as rosaries, novenas, special masses, etc. All of this appeals to man's love of the external, the elaborate, the ceremonial.

5. *Summary.* This strange yielding to human desires explains much in the Roman Catholic Church. This is one of the reasons why Protestants are so confused by Roman teachings. For side by side with the central teachings of Christianity are these strange and unbiblical doctrines. The Roman Catholic confesses the words of the Apostles' Creed just as a Lutheran does. The Church of Rome believes in the divinity of Christ, the inspiration of the Bible and many other orthodox teachings. We can rejoice in that fact.

Yet over the centuries fatal compromises have been made. This mingling of man-made truths with divine truths makes the Roman Church strong in one sense. It manages to appeal to many different classes of people and hold under one head many different ideas. Yet truth mixed with error always results in a loss of power and strength. We can learn many things from our Roman Catholic friends. But the spirit of compromise with the human element is not a characteristic we would want to copy.

Chapter Three

Beauty
Diversity
Unity

THE EPISCOPALIANS

Suppose the Lutheran Church suddenly ceased to exist! Suppose it were illegal in America to conduct a Lutheran service. In which other denomination would people of Lutheran background feel most at home?

This is a very "iffy" question and one that could provoke a lot of arguments. But undoubtedly many Lutherans would choose the Episcopal Church, and the reason for such a choice wouldn't be hard to discover.

Resemblances between the two churches are numerous. Both groups have preserved much of the historic liturgy of Christendom. The chants, the prayers, the responses are identical or similar, because in both cases they are founded on the service used by the Western Church for a thousand years before the Reformation.

Episcopal and Lutheran church buildings are also similar in their furnishings. Both use a central altar, decorated

19

with cross and candles. Both use colored hangings on altar, pulpit and lectern, changing them in harmony with the seasons of the church year. Even the vestments worn by ministers in both churches are often identical.

And, despite the use of different names, the form of church government is rather similar too. While Episcopalians have bishops and the Lutheran Church in America has none, both churches are rather democratic in their organization. Thus the pastor or rector in each church is responsible for the spiritual affairs of the congregation; the church council or vestry is responsible for the temporal affairs.

The bishop does not arbitrarily assign a pastor to a congregation in the Episcopal Church any more than a district president does so in the Lutheran Church. Nor can the bishop arbitrarily remove a pastor. The local congregation has a great deal of authority in both groups.

The resemblance is even deeper. Baptism and Holy Communion are usually administered in the same way by Lutherans and Episcopalians. Both groups continue the age-old custom of confirmation for youth and for adults. And both churches confess their faith through the use of the Apostles' Creed or the Nicene Creed. So it would seem that a Lutheran could feel right at home in the Episcopal Church.

But there's one thing that would mystify the average Lutheran, one characteristic that would come close to driving him mad. This is the peculiar tolerance of conflicting doctrines within the Episcopal fold. Though sometimes the arguments get a little tense, Episcopalians manage to keep under one big tent men who hold ideas about Christianity that are completely at variance with one another. Thus conservative and liberal Christianity both flourish. Violent Protestantism and Anglo-Catholicism that is next door to Rome—these two extremes are united in one church.

For example, some Episcopal churches practice open communion, inviting Christians of all faiths to come to the Lord's table. Other churches guard communion as closely as do most Lutheran bodies. Some Episcopal clergy participate with other Protestants in community services. Others insist that no "Protestant" preachers are really ordained at all.

Even that word "Protestant" is a fighting word for many. Some Episcopalians insist that as a part of the "Holy Catholic Church" they can not be labeled "Protestant." Other Episcopalians are proud of being a part of Protestantism, and participate in Protestant programs and activities.

This is all bewildering to a Lutheran. Common doctrine and practice have been so completely a part of our church background that we are amazed at those who don't entertain similar ideas! Lutheran synods have argued for years over points that are extremely minor, in comparison with Episcopalian divisions. It's safe to say that there's more unity among all the Lutheran bodies in America, divided though we are, than in the Episcopal Church, which is united in one organization.

How can this be? Where's the glue that keeps the Episcopal Church together? Is it simply that the leaders of the church don't care what correct teaching is? Or has the Episcopal Church found the secret of unity which has eluded other Christians? What's the explanation for such a bewildering diversity?

To find the answer, we'll do a little probing into history.

```
┌─────────────────────────────────────────────────────────┐
│                    STATISTICS                           │
│  Membership ........................  3,100,000         │
│  Congregations .....................      7,000         │
│  Clergy ............................      8,000         │
└─────────────────────────────────────────────────────────┘
```

TABLE OF COMPARISON

EPISCOPALIANS   LUTHERANS

TEACHINGS

EPISCOPALIANS	LUTHERANS
1. Accept Apostles' and Nicene Creeds.	1. Same.
2. Accept the Bible as the Word of God.	2. Same.
3. Celebrate two sacraments; some follow Roman view of seven sacraments.	3. Celebrate two sacraments: baptism and communion.
4. Believe in Real Presence in communion; some explain as only spiritual, others are close to Roman view of Transubstantiation.	4. Believe in Real Presence, that is, communicant receives bread and wine but also the body and blood of Christ.
5. Insist on apostolic succession, that is, priests must be ordained in an unbroken line back to the apostles.	5. Reject apostolic succession as a necessity for ordination. Insist that the important "succession" is to teach what the Apostles taught.

TYPE OF WORSHIP

EPISCOPALIANS	LUTHERANS
Highly liturgical. Ritual for main service fixed in "Book of Common Prayer" and not subject to change.	Liturgical but simpler. Same basic order, but followed by custom, not by rule.

GOVERNMENT

EPISCOPALIANS	LUTHERANS
An episcopal form with three ranks of clergy: bishops, priests, deacons. Congregations have considerable freedom.	No type of government prescribed. In America, the form is congregational and democratic.

CHARACTERISTICS

EPISCOPALIANS	LUTHERANS
Great appeal to wealthy, cultured, and prominent people, though also works among the downtrodden.	Strongest appeal to the middle class, though not exclusively so.

This may seem dull at first glance, though any church that once had Henry VIII as its head is not likely to have a dull history. If you want to find out why a person does certain things, you often have to investigate his past and even uncover things that happened early in childhood. The same is true of a church. So to understand the Episcopal Church in America, we have to peek into a little English history.

1. *The gradual Reformation.* Did you ever try to clean house, a little bit at a time? That's not very satisfactory. The better method is to buckle down to the work, make a determined effort to get rid of all the accumulated junk, and then settle down in a clean house for a while. That's what happened in the Lutheran Reformation. Martin Luther and his followers sought to clean the church all at once. Out went the false teachings, the pagan practices, the corrupt customs. Within the space of Luther's lifetime the essential work was finished.

But the Reformation in England didn't work that way. There was no powerful reformer like Luther in Germany or John Calvin in Switzerland or John Knox in Scotland to sweep everything aside and set up a purified church. The change was gradual. So Roman teachings, Lutheran teachings and Calvinist teachings all influenced the English church, and remained as a part of its doctrine.

Thus there's good precedent for all kinds of practice in the Episcopal Church today. At times the church has been violently "Protestant," even to the extent of mutilating statues and destroying stained glass windows in beautiful cathedrals. At other times the emphasis has been on "high-church" ceremonies, including many of the features of medieval Romanism. So each man can insist that he is not departing from Episcopal practice, though his actions may differ widely from those of his neighbor. The gradual housecleaning has its difficulties.

2. *Tolerance through weariness.* Did you ever argue with someone until you got so tired that you simply gave up and gave in? This is a favorite trick of children who keep the argument going so long that finally mother says: "All right! Do what you want to do. I don't care. All I want is a little peace and quiet!" This same weariness can come in any quarrel, even in a religious argument. And the history of England produced this tolerance through weariness.

Consider the plight of the poor preacher in England. Henry VIII broke with the Church of Rome and insisted that everyone acknowledge him as head of the church. Then Edward VI made the English Church virtually Lutheran in its teachings. Next came Mary and the swing was to Roman Catholicism. And with Elizabeth I, Romanism was out and Protestantism was back.

Nor was this the end. In the 1600s the Church of England was supreme, until the beheading of Charles I. Then the Presbyterians and Congregationalists were in control, but by 1660 the Church of England was back in the saddle. This was all very difficult for pastor and people.

One day a man was orthodox, accepted as God's spokesman. The next day he was pronounced a heretic and subject to imprisonment or even death. Many did die for their faith. But after a while everyone grew tired of wrangling. "Live and let live" became the safest philosophy. And this tolerance continues in the Episcopal Church of America.

3. The *Book of Common Prayer*. The Episcopal Church in America is not under the control of any foreign church. But one of the binding forces is the *Book of Common Prayer*. Compiled first in the reign of Edward VI, the prayerbook has been revised a number of times, but it remains one of the finest gems of English literature. Many of our Lutheran prayers are based on this prayerbook.

But the *Book of Common Prayer* is more than a work of art. Its use is required in every Episcopal Church for the main service. Men may add to the service or conduct other services, but the common pattern of worship has been a universal one. And men who use the same words in worship feel a sense of unity, regardless of their doctrinal differences.

4. *Apostolic Succession*. Now we must take a look at a little theology which is strange to Lutheran ears. This is the idea of *apostolic succession*. Rather early in the history of Christianity the idea grew up that, for a man to serve God, he had to be properly ordained. And for many this meant that he had to be ordained by a bishop who was ordained by a bishop who was ordained by a bishop, etc., back to the time of the Apostles. Such an ordination was supposed to protect the pure teachings of the church.

Sometimes this was a useful idea. False teachers could be rejected on the basis that they were not properly ordained. It's something like refusing to listen to a man because he hasn't been through college. However, at times apostolic succession had the opposite result. Rascals and false teachers were listened to *because* they had been properly ordained and therefore commanded respect.

The Church of England and the Episcopal Church in

America have retained the idea of apostolic succession. And
of course this is a binding force. Even if men didn't agree,
they recognized the ordination of each other and so felt
a common bond.

It has not been an unmixed blessing, however. For while
this theory helps to hold the Episcopal Church together, it
makes it difficult to talk union with other Christian groups
whose pastors have not been similarly ordained. Recent
unity talks with both Presbyterians and Methodists have
stumbled at this very point.

5. *The love of beauty.* One last thing must be mentioned. Stanley I. Stuber in his book *Denominations—How
We Got Them* calls the Episcopal Church "The Church
of Beauty." The name is well deserved. Out of this church
and its English antecedents have come the Book of Common Prayer and the King James translation of the Bible.
Episcopalians have sought to build beautiful cathedrals and
to encourage beautiful worship services for their people.

A TV broadcast of a church service is often an Episcopal
worship because of the pageantry and beautiful setting
and music. In a day when many Protestants (even some
Lutherans) seemed almost vying for ugliness in architecture and worship, Episcopalians were continuing their pur-
suit of beauty, and this fact also served to unify the church.

We are all partly at least a product of our past. Though
a Lutheran may be troubled by the doctrinal variation
among Episcopalians, he can understand them at least a
little when he looks at the history of the church. We can be
happy with our own unity in teaching and in commit-
ment to God's Word, even while appreciating the rev-
erent beauty emphasized by our Episcopalian neighbors.

Chapter Four

The Church
the West
Forgot

THE EASTERN
ORTHODOX

Protestant, Roman Catholic, Orthodox. We must get used to a third designation in Christian churches. For the Eastern Orthodox groups are making an imprint on our American scene.

In many cities beautiful churches with a slightly foreign look are being erected by Orthodox communities. In meetings of the World Council of Churches the voice of the eastern churches is being heard. News-flashes picture black-robed, bearded priests from Russia or from Crete delivering political pronouncements. Eastern Orthodoxy is on the march.

Yet most of us know very little about these churches. Despite the fact that Orthodox groups total close to three million members in North America, at least 100 million in the world, the average Lutheran has little conception of what the church teaches or how it came into existence.

Why is this? Why has such a sizable church made so small an impact on the American scene? Why have we only recently begun to hear about these groups? The answer will tell us a great deal about the history and the purposes of this Christian communion.

1. *It's a foreign church.* The Lutheran Church has known what it is to be a foreign church in America. Immigrants to this country organized congregations and held services in German, Norwegian, Danish, Swedish, etc. For English-speaking Americans the Lutheran church was strange and remote. People still insist that we are Germans or Swedes, even when the language barrier has been completely removed.

The Orthodox churches today are in the same position we were 50 to 75 years ago. Their people have come from Greece, Albania, Russia, Roumania, Armenia and other lands of Eastern Europe or Asia Minor. They are relatively new first- and second-generation Americans. The churches have been organized along nationalistic lines with services in languages other than English.

I once heard two Orthodox priests chanting a service. One chanted in Russian, the other in Slovak. When they came to the communion service they chanted together, this time in Greek. It was very interesting, but also very remote from the English-speaking American public.

2. *It is not an evangelistic church.* Almost everyone knows of the existence of the Jehovah's Witnesses. The members ring doorbells, they stand on the street corner, they seek to win you for their cause. If you move close to a Southern Baptist church you get the same vigorous invitation to join with that group. Churches bent on winning members at least get themselves known.

The Orthodox churches are not evangelistic in that sense.

For centuries these people have lived in countries where the membership was frozen. If you were born of Orthodox parents, you belonged to the church. If you were born of Moslem parents, you were a Moslem. No winning of converts was permitted! Only in Russia did a vigorous program of evangelism exist.

This acceptance of the status quo is a part of the heritage of all Orthodox churches. Thus you are not likely to come into contact with these people unless you seek them. Only in recent years have the clergy of the Orthodox groups begun to make their influence felt among native-born Americans.

3. *Eastern and Western Christianity have long been divided.* Did you ever watch two jealous people having a quarrel? They will find a lot of reasons for the argument, but the really basic one, jealousy, will never be mentioned. The Christian church has often suffered from the same type of quarreling, with no one willing to state the real issue at stake. The existence of eastern and western Christian churches is an example of this sort of thing.

The early church found its work centering in five great cities: Rome, Constantinople, Alexandria, Antioch and Jerusalem. Two of these, Rome and Constantinople, soon became bitter rivals. Rome had been the old head of the empire. Constantinople (called Istanbul today) became the new head.

The bishops of both cities were ambitious and not always Christian in their actions toward one another. They managed to find causes for quarreling on more than fifty topics, including the date of Easter, the belief in purgatory, the question of fasting on Saturdays in Lent, and

---

STATISTICS

Membership (U.S.) 2,800,000
Congregations 1,400
Clergy 1,700

TABLE OF COMPARISON

| ORTHODOX | LUTHERANS |

TEACHINGS

ORTHODOX	LUTHERANS
1. Accept the Nicene Creed.	1. Same, with one word added as in Western church generally.
2. Accept Bible and seven general councils as authority. Tradition valid for church.	2. Accept only the Bible as authority.
3. Celebrate seven sacraments.	3. Accept two sacraments: baptism and communion.
4. Believe in transubstantiation, that is, the bread and wine in communion changed into the body and blood of Christ.	4. Believe in the Real Presence, that is, communicant receives bread and wine but also the body and blood of Christ.
5. Believe in apostolic succession, that is, priests must be ordained in unbroken line back to apostles.	5. Reject apostolic succession as a necessity for ordination.

TYPE OF WORSHIP

ORTHODOX	LUTHERANS
Highly liturgical. Usually in the language of the people but not always so.	Liturgical but simpler in form, following the traditions and services of the Western Church.

GOVERNMENT

ORTHODOX	LUTHERANS
An episcopal form of government with bishops, priests and deacons. Patriarchs, archbishops, etc., occupy the more important bishoprics, but are not more important in theory.	No type of government prescribed. In America, the form is congregational and democratic.

CHARACTERISTICS

ORTHODOX	LUTHERANS
Great stress on drama of liturgy, on family and nation. Church often closely related to government.	Stress on the individual. Worship and life stressed equally. Church usually separated from government today.

many others. Finally in 1054, in a trivial local dispute, the Pope of Rome excommunicated the Patriarch of Constantinople and was excommunicated in return.

Even this would not have destroyed the unity of the Church because the people still felt united. But when the crusaders from the West, bent on capturing Jerusalem, went through the lands of the Orthodox churches they left behind them a bitter memory. Soldiers often antagonized the local populace, and when western soldiers sacked Constantinople, even desecrated the churches, all hope of unity was gone. The Eastern Church simply withdrew from all contact with the West and a wedge was driven into the church that is only beginning to be removed today.

4. *Eastern worship is strange to us.* Did you ever look at a church building and wonder what denomination the congregation belonged to? Most American churches are similar on the outside. Even the interiors may be alike. But the Orthodox Church has a completely different appearance. The exterior is usually almost square and there may be one or more domes in the roof. But once you step inside, you are in a different world, one that seems remote from American customs.

As one steps into an Orthodox Church he is met by a riot of color. Everywhere there is gold, mingled with brilliant blues, reds, purples. The walls and ceiling are covered with pictures or mosaics. The building seems spacious since, unless there has been a move to Americanize the structure, the church has no pews. All worshipers stand, except for a few who are old or crippled.

But the most striking difference appears in the place that we call the chancel. There will probably not be a pulpit and even the altar will not be visible. But stretching across the front of the church will be a richly ornamented screen, called an ikonostasis *(i-ḳon-o-sta-sis)*, hung with pictures and containing three doors. Behind the center door is the richly decorated altar. The whole effect of the building is exotic, taking the worshiper far away from the ordinary things of life. Many Orthodox churches bear the motto: "Standing in the temple of Thy glory, we think we stand in heaven."

The worship will seem even stranger to us than the building. The Greek or Eastern Orthodox Church has made a specialty of liturgy. Some 20 books are necessary to record all the liturgical settings used in worship. The services are lengthy, some running as long as four or five hours. This seems terribly long, especially when there are no pews in the church. However no single worshiper expects to stay for the whole service.

Think how we rush to be on time for church. If we are late we try to slip into a back pew so as not to be noticed. Not so the members of the Orthodox Church. Worshipers come and go. Each person comes in, lights a candle and places it before one of the ikons (picture of Christ or some saint) and then moves to a convenient place to hear the service. When he has heard enough, he leaves. It's as simple as that.

I once attended an Orthodox church where the choir members also came and went during the liturgy. This would drive an American choir director raving mad but the people seemed to think nothing of it.

The service is as strange to us as the customs. The liturgy seeks to act out the entire history of salvation from the time of Adam to Christ. Thus every movement and every word has a symbolic meaning. But much of the worship is conducted by the priest behind the screen. At special points there is a procession around the church with brightly garbed priests carrying the Bible or the elements for communion. The music is all sung by the choir, and it is beautiful music, usually without accompaniment. The whole effect of the service in its strange setting is bewildering and startling to Western ears. No wonder the church seems strange to us.

This stress on liturgy has been both a strength and a weakness of the Eastern churches. It reminds the worshiper constantly of the events in the history of salvation. The liturgy promotes a feeling of solidarity among the worshipers also, and has served to keep the various branches of the church reasonably well united.

On the other hand, there is little stress on individual responsibility in the church. The liturgy doesn't challenge the sinner. There is usually no sermon or at best a very brief talk; thus the layman is not moved to repentance or to deeper love for his Lord. Orthodox church leaders have become aware of these weaknesses and are stressing again the need for personal holiness.

5. *The love for the old.* Americans like things that are new. We want to be up-to-date in everything, even in our religion at times. But the pattern of the Orthodox Church is that of stress upon the old. Thus the doctrines of the church are based on the Bible and the seven general councils of the church, the last of which was held in 787 A.D. Nothing really new has been developed since that date. So the councils and traditions of the church often are the deciding factor for all truth.

This glorification of the old has preserved the Orthodox Church from some later errors in Christendom. Thus they do not believe in purgatory. They do not place as much stress on Mary as do Roman Catholics. They give the laity communion with both bread and wine. Their ministers may be married if they are married before they are ordained (although only single men and widowers can become bishops).

On the other hand, this "frozen" doctrine has also prevented the removal of what Lutherans consider error. Thus, as in the Roman Church, seven sacraments are recognized: Baptism, which is administered to children by immersion; the Eucharist or Holy Communion; Chrism or Confirmation, which is administered immediately upon Baptism; Penance; Ordination; Marriage; Extreme Unction.

"Faith" often means merely a stress on teaching rather than a real surrender to Christ. The Orthodox seeks to be "orthodox," that is, to be correct in worship and teaching, to worship and believe as the church has done for many centuries. ("Orthodox" originally meant "right worship.") This means there is resistance to every change, even to changes that might bring the church closer to the teachings of the early Christians.

No one can expect the Orthodox churches to become Americanized in the way the Methodist or Baptist or even the Lutheran has become a part of the American scene. But these representatives from Eastern Christianity are destined to play an increasingly prominent part in American church life.

Chapter Five

Young Giant
of a Church

THE METHODISTS

It may seem strange to speak of the Methodist Church as a *young* church. It has been established in most American communities for a good many years. In 1934 the Methodists celebrated their 150th anniversary as an American church body, and there were members of the church in this land even before the Revolution.

Nevertheless, compared to the Lutherans, Presbyterians or Episcopalians, Methodism is a johnny-come-lately on the world scene. For example, the Lutheran Church was more than 200 years old before the Methodists even came into existence.

Yet Methodism has become a young giant. In this country the church is second only to the Baptists in size among Protestants. Although the movement began in England,

Methodism has been called "the most characteristic American church," and the figures seem to bear out that conclusion. Of the 18 million adherents to the teachings of John Wesley, two-thirds are found on the North American continent.

How did it all happen? Why did Methodism, with such a late start among denominations, grow so rapidly? Why have Americans been so attracted to this group? The answers to those questions will tell us much about the church. Let's examine some of the elements of Methodism.

1. Sensitivity to man's needs. The Methodist church came into existence because a small group of men in England were stirred by the needs of the common people. The church began in the 18th century, often thought of as an age of elegance and reason. It was the day of Dr. Samuel Johnson, the famous author; of David Garrick, the actor; of Sir Joshua Reynolds, the painter. But it was also the age of depravity among the common people and of deadness in the church.

It's hard today to imagine the squalor of life for the common people in the 18th century. People had been forced off the farms into the factories and the mines. Liquor was cheap and men found that drink offered an easy way to forget their troubles. The church, which should have offered them guidance, was largely in the control of wealthy people, and the common man was scorned and forgotten.

Into this situation came John Wesley. He had been born in a Church of England parsonage in 1703, had been carefully trained by his devout mother, and yet could not find peace for his own soul. At Oxford he helped organize a religious club, nicknamed "the Holy Club," "the Bible Bigots," "the Bible Moths" and finally "the Methodists" (because the group believed in following regular *methods* of Bible study, prayer and holiness). But still Wesley did not feel that he was truly converted.

Strangely enough, it was a writing by Martin Luther, the *Preface to Romans,* read at a Moravian Church meeting that brought Wesley peace. Later he said in describing what took place at that meeting in Aldersgate Street, London: "I felt my heart strangely warmed. I felt I did trust in Christ, in Christ alone for my salvation; and an assurance was given me that He had taken away my sins, even mine, and saved me from the law of sin and death." (So Luther played a role in starting the Methodist Church!)

Immediately John Wesley began to preach to the common people of England. He was not revolted but challenged by the desperate needs of men. In one northern mining town when he observed the squalor and open sin, he declared: "Surely this place is ripe for the mercy of God."

His message was always the same—the need for conversion, the need for real purity and holiness of life. When the church doors were closed to him, he preached out of doors, in barns, any place he could find a crowd, and his audiences ranged from a handful to groups as large as 10,000. But always the message was directed to the personal life of the common people.

This same pattern of sensitivity to man's needs was evident in America. When settlers pushed over the mountains and established small scattered communities in Ohio, Kentucky and adjacent regions, many of the older American churches were puzzled by the situation. There weren't

```
┌──────────────────────────────────────────────┐
│                 STATISTICS                     │
│  Membership ........................ 12,400,000│
│  Congregations .....................    54,000 │
│  Clergy ............................    43,000 │
└──────────────────────────────────────────────┘
```

TABLE OF COMPARISON

METHODISTS   LUTHERANS

TEACHINGS

METHODISTS	LUTHERANS
1. Believe Bible contains Word of God; much disagreement here.	1. Accept Bible as Word of God.
2. Teach justification by faith.	2. Same.
3. Consider Baptism and Holy Communion largely symbols, not "means of grace."	3. Consider Baptism and Holy Communion God's means of conveying blessings.
4. Believe church should emphasize political and social matters.	4. Believe major stress in church must be on spiritual matters.

TYPE OF WORSHIP

METHODISTS	LUTHERANS
Formerly very free and emotional. Now tending toward a more dignified and sometimes highly liturgical pattern.	Liturgical, following classical form of the Western Church.

TYPE OF GOVERNMENT

METHODISTS	LUTHERANS
Episcopal, with bishop but no claim of Apostolic Succession. Congregations restricted in power.	No type of government prescribed, but congregational in America with much power in local church.

CHARACTERISTICS

METHODISTS	LUTHERANS
Major emphasis on Christian living with little stress on specific doctrine.	Strong stress on set doctrine. Christian life must proceed from doctrine.
Leaders in movements for reunion of Christian denominations.	Cautious about cooperation with other religious groups, without doctrinal agreement.

enough people in any place to establish a church and support a preacher.

But the Methodists responded to this challenge by sending out circuit riders who traveled from place to place bringing the Gospel to primitive backwoodsmen. John Johnson, one of the early preachers, had a circuit of 1000 miles to cover in Kentucky.

And the men who went out on these preaching missions were men of the people, men who could speak the language of the frontier. Few of them had much education but they were long on courage and devotion. Indeed, it took real courage in those days to be a preacher, for rowdies often tried to break up the services and sometimes the preacher had to whip a few members of his congregation before he could preach to them.

When America became more settled, Methodism again shifted its emphasis. Industrial development brought abuses here too, and the Methodists became the leaders in the promotion of the so-called "social gospel." They shifted their emphasis to legislation and helped to promote child labor laws, prohibition and other similar reforms. That some of this emphasis may have been one-sided does not change the fact that the Methodist Church has reacted to the needs of men more rapidly than some of the more staid Protestant groups.

2. *Dedicated workers.* Someone has said that an institution is the lengthened shadow of a man. Certainly Methodism was fortunate in the workers that it recruited from the very beginning. Wesley himself was a bear for work. It's estimated that he travelled 225,000 miles and preached 40,000 sermons in his lifetime, besides his writing and

correspondence. When you feel like complaining about the demands of church work, look at those figures again.

But Wesley was not alone. His brother Charles wrote over 6000 hymns to be used in the church gatherings (19 of them are printed in the new Lutheran hymnal). Asbury, the first Methodist bishop in America, traveled some 270,-000 miles over the rough roads of pioneer country and preached an average of a sermon a day for 45 years.

Along with this work went careful organization so that today the Methodist Church is probably the best organized, the most tightly controlled of the Protestant groups. They use a system of bishops, though only for administrative reasons and not because they deem it necessary, as the Episcopal Church does, for the preservation of the church.

3. Stress on action. We Americans like to do things, not just talk about them. Part of the appeal of Methodism lies at this point. The Methodists are busy people and were from the beginning. Doctrine never bothered Wesley very much, but he was tremendously interested in how a man lived. So the church has been characterized by a stress on Christian living, on discipline, on personal holiness. Wesley defined a Methodist as "one who lives according to the method laid down in the Bible."

Some of this emphasis has been harsh at times. Thus more stress was often given to the ban on cardplaying, dancing, smoking, theater-going and drinking than to the need for love and forgiveness. Much of this has changed in recent years but it must not be forgotten that many people like to be told specifically what not to do. So the emphasis on holiness and on action had its appeal.

4. Lack of definite doctrine. Methodism did not begin in a struggle over doctrine, and has never placed much stress on specific teachings. Wesley was so immersed in the idea of holiness that he declared: "As to all opinions which do not strike at the root of Christianity, we think and let think." A respected bishop of the church once wrote: "The distinguishing doctrine of Methodism is that it has no distinguishing doctrine."

This is not quite true. Wesley insisted on man's sinfulness, although he believed man could choose for himself good or evil. He insisted on conversion, and later Methodist preachers often taught that this must be a sudden emotional experience. And the emphasis on holiness came very close to the teaching that a man could become perfect in this life.

However, even these distinctively Methodist features have lost their force in the modern world so that Methodist doctrine today is almost impossible to define. The stress is upon living, not on believing certain truths. And we might as well admit that such an emphasis has a strong appeal to many people. They get tired of the quarrels of the church about doctrines and teaching.

But this lack of clearly defined doctrine has opened the door to many abuses. In the quarrels between liberals and conservatives that shook all American denominations, the liberals in Methodism won every time because there were no clear-cut standards. It is possible to find all shades of teaching in the church simply because no one can say, "*This* is what we believe."

5. Enthusiasm. Every now and then someone asks to sing "an old-time Methodist hymn." What he means is a hymn with vigor and pep, for Methodists have always been characterized by a certain amount of emotionalism. On the American frontier this element became so pronounced that "shouting Methodist" was almost one word. The noise and enthusiasm of the revivals left their mark on the church for a long time.

The Methodists don't shout any more. Those who desire that type of religion have largely joined the Holiness groups—which had their start in Methodism. But the enthusiasm is still there. A visitor to a Methodist church may find little liturgy in the service. He may be repelled by the informality and by funny stories from the pulpit as a part of the sermon. But he will probably get his hand shaken and he will be made to feel at home from the moment he steps in the door.

Methodists reflect this enthusiasm in their church work too. They have usually been the leaders in movements for civic betterment, for church unity, for social legislation. They have not forgotten their stress on service and the Christian life.

It's strange that Methodists and Lutherans should be so close and yet so far apart. Methodism's founder was prompted by the writings of Luther. John Wesley talked more about justification by faith than any other reformer except Luther. Yet our stress on Christian doctrine sounds strange to their ears, while their rather legalistic emphasis on holiness upsets our understanding of Christian liberty.

But we can rejoice in the example of service set by Wesley and his followers, and we can learn something about enthusiasm and action from the young giant, Methodism.

Chapter Six

Protestantism with a Difference

THE BAPTISTS

Several years ago I moved into a southern city to begin the organization of a new Lutheran church. Within 24 hours after the moving van had deposited my furniture, the local Baptist preacher knocked on my door to inquire about my church affiliation.

This is not an isolated case; it is characteristic of the aggressive work of the Baptists, particularly in the South. Such concern for the welfare of a newcomer is paying dividends in increased membership for the Baptists. Already the largest denominational bloc in American Protestantism, the Baptist church is on the march today, beginning work in store fronts, private homes, theaters, anywhere a crowd can be reached.

Some idea of Baptist growth over the years is afforded by Texas, where in 1840 there was not a single church of the Baptist faith, yet in 1955 there were 3,641 churches with 1,425,930 members.

Where do they get all this zeal? What makes the Baptist church tick? Obviously they have many consecrated, devoted workers, but Baptists don't have a monopoly on that. Moreover Baptists have some very definite handicaps in church work. Their ministry is not as well trained as that of many other groups. They don't have efficient denominational machinery, for Baptists refuse to be bound by any organization other than the local congregation. In addition, Baptists are almost hopelessly divided, and they spend considerable time battling their own groups. Yet the church is aggressive and growing. How does this happen?

Did you ever have someone tell you that you couldn't take a certain action, that you didn't dare do a certain thing? If you are a normal human being, such an injunction made you all the more determined to do what was forbidden. Perhaps some of the Baptist strength has risen from this very trait. For few religious groups have had more trouble with persecution than the Baptists.

Thus, when certain groups of Baptist leanings appeared in Germany and Switzerland during the Reformation, they were brutally suppressed. Later, similar groups appeared in England; they too felt the ire of the government. In America one of the first Baptist leaders, Roger Williams, was driven out of Salem, Mass., and forced to organize his own colony at Providence, R. I., in order to obtain freedom of religion. Through the entire colonial period sporadic persecution continued, and Baptists were among the leaders in insisting on religious liberty when the American Constitution was adopted.

This sense of persecution is still alive in Baptist thinking. Thus a Baptist book published in 1950 describes bitterly how a Lutheran bishop in Sweden forced a Baptist couple to have their child baptized, despite their wishes to the contrary. That this happened a long time ago seems to make little difference.

Even today the church watches any trend that might seem to mingle church and state in America. Baptists protested loudly when one of their own members, President Truman, sent an envoy to the Vatican. They do accept tax exemption for their churches, but only because they feel the state benefits from the presence of the church in society. Such a watch-dog attitude toward the state is usually commendable, but it also reflects Baptist feeling that they are safe only when they are aggressive and alert. The fires of persecution still rankle in their bones.

Did you ever notice that the man who feels he is different tries hard to justify himself and his views? The Russian wants to convince you of the greatness of Communism; the cat lover wants you to know that cats are better than dogs. And those different in their religious beliefs are usually equally aggressive.

There's no use denying that the Baptist Church represents a different strain in Protestantism. Indeed many Baptists refuse to be considered Protestants at all, and insist that they are not a church in the sense that Lutherans or Methodists are. This sense of difference helps to make the church aggressive to prove their viewpoint.

Consider the matter of worship. Many Christian churches have a rather free, unliturgical service. Even some Lutheran churches in the past were rather unconcerned about such

STATISTICS

```
Membership ......................... 21,000,000
Congregations ......................     91,000
Clergy .............................    115,000
```

TABLE OF COMPARISON

BAPTISTS   LUTHERANS

TEACHINGS

BAPTISTS	LUTHERANS
1. Accept the Bible as Word of God (some liberal Baptists deny this).	1. Accept Bible as Word of God, but less literalistic than conservative Baptists.
2. Accept no creeds. Each one interprets Bible for himself.	2. Accept creeds as definitions and summaries of Bible truth.
3. Practice only "believer baptism."	3. Baptize adults and children.
4. Believe immersion the only scriptural method of baptism.	4. Stress "water in the name of the Father, Son and Holy Ghost," regardless of method.
5. Believe Baptism and Holy Communion are only symbols. Call them "ordinances."	5. Believe Baptism and Holy Communion are God's means of conveying His grace. Use term "sacraments."

TYPE OF WORSHIP

BAPTISTS	LUTHERANS
Free type, according to choice of congregation or minister. Often very emotional.	Liturgical service, although not a requirement.

GOVERNMENT

BAPTISTS	LUTHERANS
Insist on congregational form as only scriptural type. Larger groupings are only voluntary.	No type of government prescribed. In America the form is congregational. General church body given much authority.

CHARACTERISTICS

BAPTISTS	LUTHERANS
Place tremendous stress on personal conversion usually with an accompanying emotional experience.	Stress individual responsibility, but education in Christian truth usually leads to more gradual "conversion."
Practice watchdog attitude regarding mixture of church and state.	Believe in "separation of church and state."

things as robes for the pastor or proper hangings for the altar. Since methods of worship are not considered binding in most Protestant groups, there has always been considerable freedom in the matter.

Not so in the Baptist church. They don't have a liturgical service because they don't *want* it. They consider it wrong, un-Christian. Thus a prominent Baptist writer says with obvious pride: "Go to the Baptist church and no altar is visible, only a communion table." The extreme Protestantism which, at the Reformation, saw only Roman Catholicism in altars and vestments and beautiful church windows is still alive among the Baptists.

Or consider the position of the Baptist minister. In general among Protestants, the pastor occupies a certain position of authority, varying from group to group. Thus Lutherans generally treasure the name "pastor" and pay high respect to the office of the ministry.

Not so the Baptists. They do often have great affection for their leaders and many churches are built around the personality of an outstanding preacher. But the minister is always one among equals. "No distinction between clergy and laity is recognized among Baptists." Each member insists on the right to interpret God's Word for himself and he feels no obligation to accept what his minister says. Indeed the preacher may be hired and fired by the congregation at will; he commands no respect by virtue of his office.

Consider that great stumbling-block, the method of baptism. For most Christian people this is a matter of indifference. Some churches let the individual choose whether he wants to be immersed or not. Even in the Lutheran Church we are willing to accept the baptism of anyone who has had water applied in the name of the Triune God, regardless of the denomination or the method used.

Not so the Baptists. While the mode of baptism is not the only important doctrine of their church, as some may think, it is a matter of tremendous importance. They are ready to defend their method at the drop of a hat and to insist that all other modes of baptism are invalid. While a few have weakened on this point in recent years, the majority of Baptists believe immersion is the only scriptural way.

Yet strangely enough, they feel that baptism is only a sign, not a channel of grace, and so is really not necessary for salvation. But if you are going to be baptized, it better be by immersion or it won't count.

This sense of being different, of having truths that other Christians have neglected, gives the Baptist a special zeal for his faith. This is more noticeable among the southern churches than their northern brothers, but it runs through their entire realm of teachings. Begin to argue religion with a Baptist and you will find that he is more than ready to tell you what he believes and why. He refuses to use a set creed to sum up his teachings, but he is very sure about them nevertheless.

One of the great blessings of the Reformation was the stress on the right of the individual to believe as his conscience guides him. Luther, standing before emperor and church officials and insisting on his right to believe the truth as he saw it, is a picture of modern man. Salvation is a personal affair, according to most Protestant groups.

No priest or church organization dare come between a man and his God.

The Baptists have accepted this truth eagerly. However, with them it has some strange notes that sound peculiar to Lutheran ears. Thus you were probably baptized as an infant. But if you had been born in a Baptist home, your baptism would have been postponed until you reached the "age of accountability." Because Baptists insist you must first accept Christ personally before you can be baptized, the teaching that God uses baptism as a means of conveying His blessings and giving the new birth to *all*, children and adults alike, is rejected by Baptists. They insist on "believer baptism."

The same stress on the individual appears when the Baptist talks about the church. He thinks only in terms of the local congregation, and even there the individual is sovereign. Larger groupings—similar to The American Lutheran Church, the Augustana Church or others in Lutheranism—these exist only as voluntary associations among Baptists. The individual is supreme and he refuses to be dominated by any larger group.

The Reformation also brought a return to the Bible. Many a Lutheran congregation proudly proclaims itself to the community as "The Church of the Word." Corrupting practices that had been introduced into Christianity were swept away by the reformers and a purified church emerged.

Once again the Baptists championed this idea, but with a difference. With them it became a desire to return to the first century, to eliminate everything that has grown up in almost 2000 years of church history. Thus for a long while many Baptists even rejected foreign mission societies —because the Bible didn't mention them. Fortunately most Baptists have changed their minds at this point.

However, the refusal to admit any possibility of gain from history has caused them to refuse any type of church organization, since the early church didn't seem too well organized. It makes them reject confirmation—the Bible doesn't mention it. By eliminating everything but the bare essentials of worship the Baptists have lost much that is good and beautiful and helpful in Christianity.

Yet even this has often been turned into an asset. The Baptist stress on New Testament times has made them avid students of the Bible. Their Sunday schools are strong and numerous, usually larger than their congregations. They maintain a Training Union program that seeks to teach all ages something about the Bible. On Sunday nights they can roll out a bigger crowd for Bible study than Lutherans can get in a dozen Sunday nights in most areas.

Protestants with a difference. That's the Baptist Church today. We might be shocked at the plainness of their churches, the lack of reverence in some of their services. We might be irritated by their aggressiveness, their assurance that they have the truth and must share it with us. But we can be thankful for the love of the Bible found among many of them and for the devotion to Jesus Christ which they are willing to express. The Baptists have come a long way since Roger Williams fled from Salem, Massachusetts, and they seem determined to go a longer way in the future.

Chapter Seven

Church
of the
Other
Reformation

THE PRESBYTERIANS

If a Christian from the first century were to return to one of our cities today, he would have difficulty with our church names. The word "Lutheran" would mean nothing to him. Neither would the name "Methodist." But he would probably recognize "Presbyterian" for it sounds like the Greek word "presbuteroi," meaning "elders." But a visitor from the first century would wonder when this term was changed into the name of a church.

Well, how *did* it happen? Where did our Presbyterian neighbors get the designation for their denomination? To understand this properly we need to know something about that "other Reformation," the movement that began in Switzerland and that produced not only the Presbyterian Church but also the Reformed, the Congregational and others.

Usually Lutherans think the Reformation began and

ended with Martin Luther. But there were other men in
other lands who also tried to purge the church of its abuses.
And Presbyterianism is the product of two of these men,
John Calvin, a Frenchman who spent his important years
in Geneva, Switzerland, and John Knox, a Scotchman who
studied under Calvin and then succeeded in making Scotland Presbyterian. Let's take a look at the characteristics
of this "other Reformation."

1. The Reformation under Calvin and Knox was more
drastic and sweeping than the Lutheran. Whenever divisions appear in the church, the first efforts seek to preserve
the common traditions of both groups. Lutheranism began
with that spirit. Thus the general worship pattern of the
Christian church was kept, but purified of certain abuses.
Stained glass windows, altars, vestments were all retained
because they had been the products of centuries of church
growth. Today the Lutheran church still has many of these
things as a part of its heritage.

But by the time Calvin and Knox began their work,
bitterness had developed. Men had been put to death for
their Protestant faith. The Roman church had hardened
in its opposition to any reforms. So the things that re-
minded men of the past were no longer considered blessings
but abominations. Out went the robes of the clergy. Out
went the candles, the crosses. Out went the altar itself.
Men were determined that nothing would remind them of
the oppression of Rome and the papacy. They determined
to go back to the beginnings of Christianity—before any
forms of worship had developed.

This drastic purging left its mark on the Presbyterians
and the other Reformed churches. For many years the

so-called Presbyterian style of architecture was the only one found in this denomination—the pulpit in the center of the church with a communion table below the pulpit and usually the choir ranged behind it. The introduction of organs into the church created a terrible row in Scotland. Organs were called "a box of whistles" and many Reformed Christians still do not like them in worship.

The experience of a little Scotch girl illustrates this dislike of things liturgical. She was taken by her mistress to a church where the choir sang beautiful chants and the organ boomed out stately music. On the way home the mistress asked the girl how she liked the service. "Oh, it was beautiful," she admitted. "But what a terrible way to spend the Sabbath." It was all show to her, not Christian worship at all.

In recent years Presbyterian churches have recaptured some of the lost forms. New buildings are being erected with altars and crosses. The plainness has given way to a new appreciation for beauty. Yet there is always a little uneasiness lest these things be thought necessary for worship. Simplicity is still a keynote of the church.

The sweeping change made itself felt in other ways too. The church before the Reformation had placed too much emphasis on the Sacraments, not enough on the preaching of the Gospel. This balance was readjusted drastically. Although Calvin believed in frequent communion, his followers were not so sure. A rigid custom of offering the Sacrament only four times a year became the rule in most places.

The pulpit in the center also reflected this changed emphasis. The sermon became the center of all worship. In Scotland, one of the laymen, called a beadle, brought the

STATISTICS

Membership **4,200,000**
Congregations **15,000**
Clergy **17,000**

TABLE OF COMPARISON

PRESBYTERIANS	LUTHERANS

TEACHINGS

1. Accept Bible as only source of faith and life.	1. Same.
2. Accept Apostles' and Nicene Creed; also Westminster Confession.	2. Accept Apostles' and Nicene Creed; also Augsburg Confession.
3. Consider sacraments as outward signs and symbols.	3. Consider sacraments as actual channels for God's blessings to us.
4. Believe that in communion the Body and Blood are received spiritually.	4. Believe in the Real Presence, that is, communicant receives bread and wine but also body and blood.

TYPE OF WORSHIP

Plain, usually unliturgical, with sermon as the climax.	Liturgical with sermon as important part of the service, not necessarily the climax.

GOVERNMENT

A system of rulership by elders, known as the presbyterian form of church government. Four levels of authority.	No type of government prescribed. In America, the form is congregational with some resemblance to the Presbyterian.

PRACTICES

Leavened bread and grape juice in communion. Distributed to worshipers in the pews.	Unleavened bread and wine in communion. Communicants come to the chancel.

Bible into the church and placed it in front of the minister each Sunday to make sure that he understood the source of his preaching.

While this custom is not followed in America, Presbyterian churches have always put a great stress on preaching and have produced many outstanding preachers. The worship service leads to the sermon and as soon as it is finished the service is closed quickly with a short prayer, a benediction and perhaps a hymn. Baptism and Holy Communion are retained, though they are not considered means of grace but outward signs of a spiritual blessing which must be received through faith.

2. This second Reformation was also a systematic one. Martin Luther was a great thinker but his teachings grew out of his personal struggle for assurance of salvation. Such a personal experience is not inclined to be systematic and orderly. Even our Lutheran standard of faith, the Augsburg Confession, was not written by Luther but by his friend, Philip Melanchthon.

John Calvin was also a man who felt deeply. But he had a systematic mind, moved by logic and reason. Perhaps he was the most logical and systematic teacher that the Christian Church has ever developed. Presbyterianism took over this careful development of truth and this has been characteristic of the church from its beginning. Thus four principles are usually stressed by Presbyterians as the core of Biblical teaching:

1. The undivided sovereignty or rulership of God in His universe.
2. The sovereignty of God in salvation.

3. The sovereignty of the Scriptures in faith and conduct.
4. The sovereignty of the individual conscience in the
   interpretation of the Word of God.

Presbyterians are still concerned about doctrine. Incoming members are expected to give a statement of their faith, although sometimes this practice has fallen into disuse. The church sums up its teachings in the Westminster Confession, drawn up by 151 teachers and laymen in England in the middle of the 17th century. The confession is logical and clear. In recent years quarrels have broken out in the church between liberals and conservatives, but no one thinks doctrine unimportant. The logic of John Calvin still moves his followers.

There was one place where the logic created a terrible problem. Men have always wrestled with the problem of how God can have all power and want all men to be saved and yet some are not saved. Calvin had to find a solution for this and he finally decided that God had predestined some to be saved and some to be damned. While this seems a rather remote doctrine today, there was a time when it was a red-hot issue in the Christian Church.

Calvin's solution seemed so logical—and yet so terrible. Predestination was a disturbing problem for the Presbyterians for many years. In recent years there has been a change. In 1903 the church declared: "Men are fully responsible for their treatment of God's gracious offer (of salvation) and . . . no man is hindered from accepting it and . . . no man is condemned except on the ground of his sin." No Lutheran would quarrel with this position today.

Perhaps the genius for organization and system which

characterized John Calvin and his followers is best shown in the Presbyterian form of church government. The church is governed by elders or presbyters, hence the name. Each congregation is ruled by the *session,* which is composed of the pastor (or *teaching* elder) and the lay representatives (or *ruling* elders). Over the session is the *presbytery,* composed of ministers and representative ruling elders in an area. The next division is the *synod,* and topping the whole structure is the *general assembly,* a representative body of the entire church.

Presbyterianism is often called a church ruled by committees. The organizational lines are clear and precise. The structure is similar to our own Lutheran church pattern in this country, but we have never claimed any special Biblical basis for any system of church government. The Presbyterians, however, insist that theirs is the type employed in the New Testament.

This same careful system shows itself in many ways in the life of the church. Thus the Christian life is carefully organized and occasionally becomes rather legalistic. Many of the so-called Sunday blue laws in America had their origin in the rigid rules for the Sabbath which the Scotch brought to this country.

3. Paradoxically, despite the efforts at strict control, the "second Reformation" also stressed the freedom of the common man. Lutheranism adapted itself to the form of government prevailing in each Lutheran land. But Presbyterianism was not so mild. From the beginning a tradition of resistance to autocratic authority was instilled in the church. Thus John Knox told Queen Mary of

Scotland: "If princes exceed their bounds, madam, they may be resisted and even deposed." Those were bold words in that day.

Presbyterians coming to America brought with them this resistance to tyranny. The only clergyman to sign the Declaration of Independence was a Presbyterian. Horace Walpole in England's Parliament spoke scornfully of the American rebellion as "this Presbyterian revolution," and the Scotch immigrants who fought for independence gave his words a ring of truth.

Whenever there has been need for resistance against tyranny, Presbyterians have played their part. Their ministers have spoken out boldly against corruption and wrongs in government. Sometimes it may have seemed to others like political meddling, but it is a part of the tradition of the church to resist evil in high places. Both in Scotland and in America, the church began with a struggle against political power; it has never forgotten this fact.

It seems rather obvious that there are many places where Lutherans and Presbyterians agree. This is to be expected, for both churches profess a strong love for the Scriptures and for careful study of Christian doctrine. While there are differences, due to the different circumstances and spirit between the Lutheran and the Calvinistic Reformation, there are many places where we can rejoice together in a common acceptance of the truths of God's Word.

The New Old Church

Chapter Eight

THE UNITED CHURCH OF CHRIST

The newest denomination in America is the United Church of Christ, which came into existence June 25, 1957, in Cleveland. In fact, the organization is so new that the members are still writing a constitution for governing the group. But some of the congregations belonging to this new denomination have been in existence for 300 years. So the United Church of Christ can very properly be called "a new old church."

Any way you look at this denomination it seems strange and unusual. Can you imagine New England Puritans sitting side by side with German Lutherans? That is practically what is happening in the United Church of Christ. For the first time in American church history, two groups with different national backgrounds and with different forms of church government have merged into one organization.

For some people the United Church of Christ is a monstrosity, a denomination composed of such strange parts that it cannot stand for anything or mean anything. On the other hand, many regard this new merger as the most forward step in American church history, a move toward destroying denominational barriers which have plagued the Protestant Church. Time will tell which view is correct.

The simplest way to understand this new group is to look at the four strands that have been woven together into one. Two mergers preceded this one. In 1931 the General Council of Congregational and Christian Churches came into being. And in 1934 the Evangelical and Reformed Church was born. Thus there are four parts of the new United Church of Christ: Congregationals, Christians, Evangelicals, and Reformed. Let's take a look at each segment and see how it fits into this new venture.

1. *The Congregational Church.* Almost every American is familiar with the style of church building known as colonial. This is the white frame building with pillars in front. Inside, the pews and chancel furniture are plain and usually white. The simplicity of this building has made it a favorite with many people and it has spread from New England into most parts of America.

Originally this New England style colonial church went with a particular style of Christianity known as Congregationalism. This was the religion of the Puritans. It arose in England as a challenge to the absolute control of bishops and kings over the church. In America it was a faith that was in keeping with pioneer times—simple, plain, freedom-loving, individualistic. As a matter of fact, Congregationalism became the state church in parts of New England and remained so even after the formation of the United States of America.

Two things checked the growth of the Congregational Church and kept it largely a sectional group. First, a split in the church took place in 1825 when the Unitarian wing withdrew, taking with it the oldest and largest churches of the denomination.

In addition, Congregationalism had entered into an agreement with the Presbyterians to stay out of the newly developing west. This agreement was cancelled in 1852 but the Congregationals insist that they lost 2,000 potential churches by this agreement.

Modern Congregationalism is very different from the early New England variety. The Puritans were rigid in doctrine, preaching a stern message of heaven and hell, of God's love and God's punishment, punishment even for little children. Modern Congregationalism seems to exhibit the reverse emphasis. Doctrinal standards are not at all rigid. Congregationalism has often been called the inter-denominational denomination since it has always been willing to cooperate with all other church groups and has been a leader in inter-church movements.

But one factor has remained unchanged—the emphasis on the congregation as its own authority in all matters. Strictly speaking, Congregationalism has never been a denomination but an association, for each church retains the right to make its own decisions as to doctrinal and practical matters. This has created difficulty for the present merger; some Congregational churches have refused to enter the United Church of Christ.

```
STATISTICS
Membership ......................... 2,200,000
Congregations ......................    8,200
Clergy .............................    8,800
```

TABLE OF COMPARISON

THE UNITED CHURCH   LUTHERANS

TEACHINGS

1. No prescribed creeds. A new statement of faith adopted but not binding. Teaching may vary from one congregation to another.
2. Most accept the Trinity, though the statement is vague.
3. Most accept sacraments as signs of God's blessing.
4. Believe Christ's presence is symbolized in communion.
5. Most rely on Christ's redemption for salvation.

1. Accept the Apostles' Creed and the Nicene Creed. All congregations teach in accord with Lutheran confessions.
2. Accept the Trinity.
3. Accept sacraments as the channels of God's blessing.
4. Believe in the Real Presence of Christ in Communion.
5. Teach that man is saved by God's goodness, shown in Christ's redemption.

TYPE OF WORSHIP

No set form of worship, but usually non-liturgical.

Worship is liturgical, but not made binding on churches.

GOVERNMENT

Strictly congregational, but some problems remain as to the power to be exercised by authorities of the church body.

No type of government prescribed. In America congregational but with powers delegated to church body.

CHARACTERISTICS

Strong stress on Christian living; with a weak emphasis on doctrine. Strong emphasis on church unity and co-operative movements.

Strong emphasis on doctrine, with the Christian life supposed to proceed from faith in Christ.
Inclined to be cautious about cooperative movements.

2. *The Christian Church.* The name "Christian Church" has been used by a number of different groups and it is easy to get them confused. However they all grew out of a strange movement in the early part of the last century.

Did you ever get tired of the different denominations and wish they would all stop talking about doctrines and just go back to the Bible? Most of us have felt that way from time to time. So did a lot of people during the early 1800s. The religious groups in America had been spending more time fighting each other than in seeking to reach souls for Christ.

Certain people came to the conclusion that it would be better if creeds and doctrines were abolished and everybody went back to the Bible. It sounded like a beautiful dream. And that's about all it was, for the result of this movement was the creation of several new denominations, rather than the abolishment of the old ones.

One of these new groups took the name of "American Christian Convention" and used the name "Christian" for its congregations. Just as in Congregationalism, these local Christian congregations were independent. The doctrinal position was very broad, with even such teachings as the Trinity and the divinity of Christ regarded as subjects on which individual members might differ. In 1931 this group merged with the Congregational Church, and the General Council of the Congregational and Christian Churches came into being.

3. *The Reformed Church.* Did you know that there was once a proposal offered to make German the official language in America? It actually happened in Pennsylvania,

and it isn't hard to see why such an idea should originate in that state. In the early 1700s thousands of immigrants from Germany and Switzerland poured into Pennsylvania, moved by the intolerance of Europe plus the tolerance and the opportunities offered by America. These people produced the strange dialect and the customs known as "Pennsylvania Dutch."

Many of these immigrants were Lutheran, and Pennsylvania is still a strongly Lutheran state. But there were also many people belonging to a church known as Reformed. They held a faith which was a combination of the teachings of Luther and those of John Calvin, the reformer who worked in Geneva, Switzerland.

Reformed teaching was close to Lutheranism in many ways. Both groups had a deep love for the Word of God. Both believed in the same Lord and Savior. Both instructed their young people by the use of catechisms. Because of similarities and also because of a common language, Reformed and Lutheran congregations often shared the same church building and even the same pastor.

But there were differences too. The meaning of Christ's words in Holy Communion divided the two groups, the Lutherans insisting that Christ was truly present, the Reformed clinging to the idea that Christ was symbolized in the Sacrament. Also, Lutheranism tended to stress sound doctrine; Reformed teachings put more emphasis on Christian living.

So there was no uniting of the two churches. For a while the German Reformed group existed under the direction of the Dutch Reformed. Then in 1793 it became a separate denomination. The membership was strongly concentrated in Pennsylvania and Ohio.

4. *The Evangelical Church.* The name "evangelical" stresses the fact that a church preaches the gospel. Thus most Lutheran congregations have this word in their official names. But the existence of a separate group using this word as a denominational name occurred because of the actions of a German king, Frederick William III of Prussia. The king grew tired of having two churches in his realm, the Lutheran and the Reformed. So in the early 1800s he ordered them to merge into one. Many Lutherans resisted this action but there were others who decided to go along. Originally the church was about 80% Lutheran.

When members of the merged church came to America, they decided to form a similar group which came to be known as the Evangelical Synod of North America. This organization appeared in 1840. Many of the churches here too were Lutheran and even carried that name. Luther's Catechism was used by many, while others employed the Reformed or Heidelberg Catechism. The church rules provided that wherever the two catechisms disagreed, such matters were to be settled by Scripture, but also that liberty of conscience must be present in the church.

It was inevitable that the Reformed Church and the Evangelical Synod should be drawn together—they had common ideas and background. The two churches became the Evangelical and Reformed Church in 1934, though the church-wide boards were not actually merged until 1940. The motto of the church indicated its pattern rather well—"in essentials unity, in non-essentials liberty, in all things charity."

5. *These are the four strands* that now make up the

new denomination, the United Church of Christ. It does seem a strange group to be drawn together. Lutherans and Puritans, descendants of Germans and Englishmen, New Englanders and Pennsylvania Dutch.

Yet one common thread seems to run through the four churches. In every case there is a stronger stress on Christian living, on service, than on doctrine. Thus the new statement of faith drawn up by the four bodies in 1959 says nothing about the Virgin Birth and speaks of Jesus as "the man of Nazareth, our crucified and risen Lord," which is a rather mild assertion of His divinity. But the same statement says that God calls us into His Church:

"to accept the cost and joy of discipleship,
 to be his servants in the service of men,
 to proclaim the gospel to all the world and resist the powers of
  evil,
 to share in Christ's baptism and eat at his table,
 to join him in his passion and victory."

This statement of faith is called a testimony, not a test, and no one is bound by it nor compelled to use it.

There have always been people who have dreamed of a creedless church, a group where the emphasis is on doing, not on believing. The United Church of Christ seems to be that church. As such it represents a new thrust in Christendom, an effort to do God's bidding without first coming to a complete statement of what that bidding is.

The whole Christian Church will watch this new organization with interest. Will it lose the old elements of truth that each of the churches had and become a vaporous thing? Or will each section make the other stronger? Only time will provide the answer.

Chapter Nine

The Church
with a
Dream

THE DISCIPLES OF CHRIST

Did you ever notice that many people like to dream
about the glories of the past? "The good old days" have
an almost irresistible appeal for them. Somehow it seems
life was simpler, easier, more agreeable in former times.

Christians too are often captured by this mood. Indeed,
all of us feel a little of this love for the past when we read
in Acts the description of those first Christians: "Now
the company of those who believed were of one heart and
soul, and no one said that any of the things which he
possessed was his own, but they had everything in common" (Acts 4:32). What a beautiful picture that is!

One denomination in America owes its existence to this
love for the past, this desire to get back to the time when
life was simpler and less complicated. The Disciples of
Christ, whose local churches are often called "Christian,"
came into existence because men were moved by a longing
for the simple, primitive Christian faith.

This denomination had its origin almost exclusively in
America—it's a native-born product. But you can't under-

stand the Disciples of Christ without knowing the dream that brought them into being.

1. *The Dream*. Once upon a time the Christian church existed without written creeds. At first there were simply believers united by a common faith. The statements of Christian doctrine came later, when men began to argue over the truth. The Apostles' Creed, the Augsburg Confession of the Lutheran Church, and all other theological statements came after the church was formed and the Bible was written.

Men have often said: "Let's get rid of these creeds, these man-made statements, and go back to the Bible!" The motto became: "No creed but Christ." The principle was announced: "Where the Bible speaks, we speak; where the Bible is silent, we are silent." These were a part of the dream and are still part of the faith of the Disciples of Christ.

The second part of the dream followed logically. There once was a time when there weren't any Lutherans, any Presbyterians, any Roman Catholics. All Christians once were one. So, maybe if all creeds could be swept away, if all denominations could be eliminated, the church could be united again as it was at the first. This was the goal of those who began the Disciples and they stubbornly insisted that they were not a denomination, not another separate church but simply the beginning of a return to first-century Christianity.

It was a beautiful dream. It isn't hard to see how it captured the imaginations of many people and still has attraction today. The Disciples began at a time when denominational quarrels were bitter and ugly. The existence of so many different churches in early America (whereas each European country had only a few) brought out the worst in many hearts. For example, one of the leading revivalists of this period, speaking about those who opposed him, called his fellow ministers . . .

. . . hirelings, caterpillars, letter-learned Pharisees, hypocrites, varlets, seed of the serpent, foolish builders whom the devil drives into the ministry, dead dogs that cannot bark, blind men, dead men, men possessed of the devil, rebels and enemies of God.

Other attacks were even worse. No wonder men were captured by the dream of a creedless church where Christians could live together in simplicity and love.

2. *The Dreamers.* The people who became "Christians" or "Disciples" came from the ranks of the Methodists, the Baptists and the Presbyterians. But the most prominent leaders were originally Presbyterian—Barton W. Stone and Alexander Campbell.

Stone was a minister near Cane Ridge, Kentucky, in the period after the Revolutionary War when men pushed over the mountains and settled the Bluegrass state. In that pioneer time, around 1800, great revivals were held in the wilderness. People came for miles and stayed for a week or more. Often three or four preachers of different denominations would be preaching at the same time. The hearers would be so overcome that some would fall over in a dead faint, while others would shout and sing or even begin to bark like dogs.

Stone assisted at the great Cane Ridge revival in his own parish when 20,000 people attended. But he and many others couldn't see why preachers of different groups

```
┌─────────────────────────────────────────────────┐
│              S T A T I S T I C S                  │
│  Membership  .......................  3,800,000  │
│  Congregations  ....................     26,000  │
│  Clergy  ...........................     20,000  │
└─────────────────────────────────────────────────┘
```

TABLE OF COMPARISON
DISCIPLES   LUTHERANS

TEACHINGS

DISCIPLES	LUTHERANS
1. Reject all creeds and summaries of faith.	1. Use Apostles' Creed, catechism, etc. to summarize teachings of the Bible.
2. Faith, followed by repentance — both viewed as man's work.	2. Repentance, followed by faith— both viewed as work of the Holy Spirit.
3. Original sin or evil nature of man rejected.	3. Original sin confessed as a part of man's nature.
4. Holy Communion only a memorial supper.	4. Holy Communion a memorial but also the giving by Christ of His body and blood.
5. Usually unionistic, that is, seeking to work with other denominations.	5. Cautious in approach to other groups, feeling that the truth might suffer.

TYPE OF WORSHIP

Unliturgical, although some are beginning to use form in worship. Holy Communion celebrated each Sunday. Some churches refuse to use musical instruments.	Liturgical. Holy Communion celebrated less frequently, although tendency is to increase frequency. Musical instruments used.

GOVERNMENT

Completely congregational. Each group or congregation is independent but cooperates with others as it desires.	Congregational in America but authority for certain tasks delegated to general body.

CHARACTERISTICS

Strong emphasis on the Bible, but no formal training given members and standards for joining are simple.	Bible-centered. Insists on careful training of members before they are officially received.

should preach at the same revivals while the people stayed divided into separate denominations. So he began to gather people into churches simply called "Christian," with supposedly no denominational bias.

Alexander Campbell came to America from Scotland, following in the footsteps of his father. Father and son were disgusted to find divisions among the Presbyterians in America, reflecting quarrels that applied only to Scotland. So they began to agitate for a restored New Testament church, freed from such artificial matters. For a while they associated with the Baptists but later withdrew, taking many Baptists with them. Alexander Campbell was a skillful writer and a gifted debater. On one occasion he debated with another minister at Lexington, Kentucky, for 18 days and the famed Henry Clay served as moderator.

Campbell and Stone soon recognized that they had a common interest and a common idea and so they united their followers in a loose organization in 1833, although they insisted that they weren't a denomination, only a fellowship of Christian believers.

Some difficulty occurred about the name. Campbell liked "Disciples of Christ," while Stone preferred "Christian." So both names are still used today, with the denominational name being Disciples of Christ, the local churches normally labelled "Christian," and one group of congregations calling themselves "Church of Christ." (One group of Stone's followers united with the Congregationalists in 1931, and is now a part of the new United Church of Christ—see preceding chapter.)

3. *The Details of the Dream.* It is easy to say, "Where

the Bible speaks we speak, where the Bible is silent we are silent." Unfortunately, it isn't that simple. The Disciples soon found that they had to indicate just what they understood the Bible to say. Despite their reluctance to adopt a creed, there has gradually come into existence a rather clear-cut statement of Christian truth. As the details of this dream of a creedless church were spelled out, the following came to be a part of the framework for reuniting the churches:

The Bible is considered the source and key of all Christian truth. However, for Christians, only the New Testament is considered binding. In the New Testament the pattern for the church is given, so this is all that Christianity needs. Obviously many quarrels in the church could be avoided by this approach, but not all are ready to give up the Old Testament as a source of truth.

The steps by which a man becomes a Christian are: faith, repentance, baptism, the forgiveness of sin and the gift of the Holy Spirit. There is no original sin in man's heart. Man is able to come to faith in God's Word by himself—without any outside help or any emotional experience. This view has strong appeal to those who dislike emotional revivals. It also appeals to those who don't like to be told about their own deep-seated sinfulness. However, this view of a man's approach to Christianity would be challenged by almost every other denomination.

The sacraments have long been sources of division in the Christian Church. The Disciples after some discussion came to accept Baptism by immersion as the way of entrance into the church, although they have never really agreed as to whether Baptism by sprinkling in another church is acceptable or not.

Holy Communion was accepted as a memorial supper, not a sacrament, and is administered each Sunday in the church. Grape juice and cubes of bread are passed to worshipers in the pews. Sometimes a service has no sermon, but the Lord's Supper is always celebrated.

Two problems caused great anguish in the church. First, could the church use organs for the worship service? Second, could or should the church organize missionary societies for sending foreign missionaries? Since neither of these is mentioned in the New Testament, strict members of the church insisted that both were to be avoided. More liberal members felt that these two things were not forbidden and so could be used to advance the church's work.

The dispute grew so bitter that many of the congregations, located largely in the South, banded together as Churches of Christ and continue to use that name. It is strange to hear these people sing hymns with no accompaniment, but practice has made them very skillful in such singing.

4. *The Stern Realities.* Dreams are often valuable, but we always have to awake to the realities of life. Unfortunately, the realities have not completely agreed with the dream of Stone and Campbell. Today, despite all efforts to avoid the unpleasant fact, the Disciples of Christ have become another American denomination—in fact a pair, if the Churches of Christ are considered separately. Despite the goal set by the founders, not a single denomination disappeared. The divisions of the church were not healed.

Nor was the goal of "no creed but Christ" maintained. The Disciples were forced to decide what they believed in many matters and every time such a decision was reached, that statement became a creed, like it or not. On the other hand, the absence of formal statements opened the door for liberal attacks on Biblical Christianity. In the areas where the church had not spoken, false notions regarding the Trinity, the Divinity of Christ and other basic teachings found an opening and an opportunity to grow and to undermine. The split between conservatives and liberals has been sharp in this church because of the absence of any really binding doctrinal guides.

However, there have been other blessings not really envisioned by the first dreamers. The Disciples have been leaders in Bible study because they have centered their church on an understanding of the New Testament. Colleges founded by groups in the church have enriched the church through their work.

Members of this denomination have also been leaders in promoting greater unity and cooperation among Christians. When it became evident that the great dream of uniting all churches by getting them to renounce their creeds had failed, leaders in the church began to explore other possibilities for bringing Christians closer together.

Today some Disciples call themselves "A denomination that hopes to die." Their continued existence is a witness to the church of the longing that Christians have to be united into one church again. Regardless of our attitude toward their doctrinal positions, we cannot help but feel drawn to them in their desire for a reunited church.

Someone has said: "The Disciples don't have preachers, they have editors." We are all indebted to this church for their emphasis on the printed word. The Disciples grew through their publications. The widely read "Christian Century" was once a publication of the Disciples of Christ. Long before Jehovah's Witnesses discovered the secret, the Disciples were using printer's ink to let people know what they believed.

Theirs has been a rich history. The largest denomination purely American born may not have realized its dream, but it has indeed made its imprint on reality.

Chapter Ten

An American Success Story

THE MORMONS

The American success story is a familiar one. It begins with a young man in dire poverty. Then, step by step, he climbs the ladder of success despite almost crushing opposition. At the end of the story the poor boy is prosperous, happy, respected by all. In fiction and in real life this pattern is recreated hundreds of times. And although the comparison may seem a strange one, the Mormons or Latter-Day Saints (as they call themselves) conform to the American success story in all its details.

Consider the pattern of growth. Mormonism began with six members in 1830. These first believers were poor, almost uneducated. Yet the church grew until today the various branches of Mormonism claim more than a million adherents. The church is prosperous, owning businesses and farms. It has achieved a level of respectability despite the former stigma of polygamy. During the Eisenhower years, a Mormon elder sat in the Cabinet of the United States government.

Moreover, this growth has been achieved in the face of great difficulties, thus also paralleling the American success story. The Latter-Day Saints are the only church group ever attacked by the United States army, the only denomination that provoked the U. S. Congress to pass specific legislation suppressing a religious teaching. The Mormons were driven from Ohio, from Missouri, from Illinois before they found a haven in Utah.

Yet today their beautifully trained choir sings sacred numbers that find their way to the top of the hit parade. If earthly success, despite difficulties, were the only measure of a religion, Mormonism would rank high among the world's faiths. Let's see how it all happened.

1. *The appeal of the strange,* the unknown. Most of us have a sneaking liking for that which is strange, improbable and mysterious. We get a little bored with that which is staid and matter of fact. The flying saucer mania is a good example of this human tendency. And from the very outset Mormonism appealed to many people because of its bizarre origin and teachings.

The story of its beginning is hard to equal even in the realm of deliberate fiction. Joseph Smith, the founder, claimed to be disturbed by the divergent claims of various denominations in America. While praying for guidance, God the Father and Jesus Christ appeared to him and told him not to join any church, since none of them taught the truth. Later an angel showed Smith where some gold plates were hidden in a hillside near Palmyra, New York.

By the aid of some magic spectacles Joseph Smith was

```
STATISTICS
Membership ......................... 1,600,000
Congregations .......................     4,300
Clergy ...............................     4,000
```

TABLE OF COMPARISON

MORMONS   LUTHERANS

TEACHINGS

MORMONS	LUTHERANS
1. Vague on Trinity. Seem to believe in many gods.	1. Belief in the Triune God.
2. Belief in new revelations from church at any time.	2. Belief in New Testament faith "once for all delivered."
3. Salvation through following Christ's example.	3. Salvation is God's gift received through faith in Christ as Redeemer.
4. Accept Bible, Book of Mormons, and other sources of authority.	4. Accept only the Bible as authority.
5. Reject original sin. Children sinless until eight.	5. Believe all people born in sin.
6. Reject infant baptism but baptize for dead. Immersion only.	6. Baptize infants. Do not reject any method of baptism.
7. Communion only a symbol. Bread and water used.	7. Believe communicant receives Body and Blood of Christ as well as bread and wine.

TYPE OF WORSHIP

No liturgy. Communion celebrated every Sunday. No trained ministry to lead service.	Liturgical worship. Communion celebrated at chosen times. Ordained ministry usually leads worship service.

CHURCH GOVERNMENT

Highly organized and effective lay participation. Real power in officials of church.	Congregational form of government. Real power in local congregation, though some authority delegated to elected officials.

able to translate the plates and thus write the Book of Mormon. This book or series of books claimed that the American Indians were descendants of the lost tribes of Israel. Supposedly, Jesus made an appearance to them after His resurrection and founded a church in America. Later the true worshipers were all killed, but the golden plates were inscribed and buried to preserve the story of the true faith.

This is strange enough but it isn't all of the story. Joseph Smith continued to receive heavenly visitors, including John the Baptist and the apostles Peter, James and John. Two other books of Mormon teaching were produced by the founder, *Book of Doctrines and Covenants* and *Pearl of Great Price*. In addition, various pronouncements or revelations were made from time to time, including one that taught polygamy. Mormonism has continued to insist that special revelations can be given by leaders of the church at any time, although no important revelations have appeared for many years.

This strange story of Joseph Smith and the odd writings that he produced has had an appeal for many people who are looking for something new. The Book of Mormon itself is so dull that Mark Twain called it "chloroform in print." But the presence of a separate series of revelations which are supposed to "support but not supplant the Bible" has an allure for some. Mormonism accepts the Bible "insofar as it is correctly translated," but such a viewpoint opens the door to strange notions whenever Bible statements contradict Mormon teachings.

Actually it's hard to define just what the Mormons do believe since the church has passed through many phases in its brief history. It's possible to find statements in the classical Christian tradition made by its leaders, but also possible to discover declarations that seem to teach the existence of many different gods. In recent years, as Mormons have come in closer contact with various Christian groups, the doctrine has tended to take on a rather conservative Christian veneer, though some strange teachings still remain.

Two of the most intriguing doctrines are baptism for the dead and sealing for eternity. According to Mormon teaching, people who have died without being converted can become believers in the next world but they cannot be baptized since they now lack bodies. So living Mormons get baptized for their ancestors and dead friends. As a result of this, the church maintains elaborate lists of family trees and searches old records to make sure baptism has been administered for all the dead.

Marriage has always been a peculiar spot in Mormon teaching. Polygamy was once the practice of the church but was abolished under pressure of the federal government. Actually only about 10% of the Mormons were polygamists since it was too expensive and it also went against the grain of people (even Mormons) in the 19th century. However, the church recognizes (1) marriage for this world and (2) marriage for all eternity. Special services must be held in a Mormon temple for the sealing for eternity. Thus a man may have one wife for this world and another in the next.

There is no doubt that the strange element in Mormonism has helped it to grow. Even today there are secret rites which are administered only in the Mormon temples and not even every Mormon is permitted to enter such a place. Nothing too unusual seems to occur during these ceremonies but the element of strangeness and secrecy appeals to many.

2. *The power of persecution.* The young man climbing toward success is often spurred on by difficulties in the way. Similarly Mormonism owes some of its present strength to the persecution endured by the first believers. There is an old saying that the blood of the martyrs is the seed of the church. What is often overlooked is that it is part of human nature to resist compulsion, regardless of the right or wrong of the issue at stake. When parents say "no" children often say "yes," and the same principle applies to people generally in religious matters.

There's no doubt that the Mormons did suffer cruelly at the hands of religious bigots, though sometimes they courted trouble too. The first group was driven out of Kirtland, Ohio, then out of Independence, Mo. For a time they settled in Nauvoo, Illinois, and prospered there. But trouble broke out again and this time Joseph Smith and his brother were killed. The upshot was that the church came under the capable leadership of Brigham Young, although a section refused to follow him.

The opposition could have done nothing sillier than killing Joseph Smith. Before this time the church was beginning to stir with discontent. Smith was a better mystic than he was a leader. But the killing of their prophet made the Mormons determined to show the world their courage. They made the terrible trek to Utah and there established headquarters. Even the struggle over polygamy, during which many of the leaders were forced into hiding, couldn't shake Mormon determination. Persecution and hardship proved more a blessing than a curse to these people. Like the typical hero in the success story, they rose above their difficulties.

3. *The talent for organization.* But even strange doctrines and persecution are not sufficient to make a church a success. We must also note the structure of the church as Joseph Smith planned it. For Mormonism is admirably designed to encourage the participation of all the members and to keep the members involved in the work of the church.

According to Mormonism, there are two divinely instituted orders or groups of priests named after Aaron and Melchizedek. Each order has three grades and a boy of 12 may begin by being a deacon in the Aaronic group. Step by step the Mormon can advance in his church, with each step involving some new duties. There are no paid ministers in a congregation; the work is all carried on by the lay members.

The organization reaches to the very top. Each church is known as a ward, with a group of congregations being known as a stake. Over all the stakes is a group known as the 12 apostles and above them is the president with two assistants. The striking thing is that the church functions with few paid officials. Thus at services in the local church different members take turns speaking and preaching. In addition, young men are required to give one or two years of their life in missionary service if the church demands it; they are not paid for their work either.

The church also seeks to reach into every phase of the member's life. The local church is set up for worship, teaching and recreation. Members are to find their whole interest here. But it works both ways. Mormons are required to tithe and this money is sent to church head-quarters. Then if people are unemployed or in need, the church takes care of its own. During the depression few Mormons were on the relief rolls of the government. Their church took care of them.

However, commendable as this efficient organization may be, it also indicates the weakness of Mormonism from a Lutheran point of view. Far more basic than the odd doctrines of the church is the stress on salvation by works. Each Mormon serves his God by doing the things required of him. Thus the steps up in the priesthood are achievements, works which the members do. The same emphasis is given to the tithe and to rules against alcohol, tobacco, coffee and tea.

It cannot be denied that the Mormons do speak about Christ, that they even refer in a vague way to His atonement for sin. Yet they do not believe in original sin and they really view Christ as a new lawgiver who has shown us the way to win salvation by keeping the laws.

Indeed, this striving on the part of man doesn't even cease at the end of this life for there are levels in heaven too. And while the church is rather vague on this point, it seems to believe that some day all souls will be saved.

This is the tragedy of the success story. Such energy has been expended, such work has been done and yet the free blessing of forgiveness has been covered over. Even though the Bible is still read in the Mormon Church, the peculiar doctrines tend to crowd out the teachings of Scripture.

Nevertheless we can admire and learn from these Latter-Day Saints. Certainly we can learn the importance of active participation on the part of every member. We do not need to get rid of our ministers but we can learn to assist them by taking full part in the program of the church. And as young people we might measure our devotion to the Lord against the action of the young Mormon who gives a year or two of his life, without pay, to serve his church.

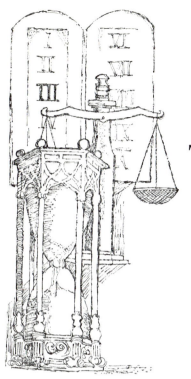

Chapter Eleven

The Church
That Looks
Two Ways

ADVENTISTS

Every now and then someone predicts that the world is going to come to an end very soon. Some of these prophets even venture to name the exact date for this catastrophic event. Usually a few people get excited, most of us say "Crackpot," and when the date is past the whole matter is forgotten.

But in the year 1844 there occurred one of the strangest events in American church history—a man named a date, failed in his attempt and yet indirectly started a large American denomination. The man was William Miller, a farmer in New York and later a Baptist preacher.

Miller made a diligent study of the prophecies of Daniel

and Revelation, then came to the conclusion that the end of the world was very near. He found followers in a number of churches and his disciples were dubbed "Millerites," though they stayed in their own denominations. Finally, after venturing several guesses, Miller predicted that the world would definitely end on Oct. 22, 1844.

This prophecy created a great deal of excitement. Some of the Millerites sold their property and gave the money away, which wasn't particularly charitable if the world was about to end anyway. Other believers settled all their business accounts and spent their time in prayer. Some even donned white robes and stood on a hillside, waiting for the Lord to take them to heaven. Their embarrassment the next morning must have been acute.

The failure of the prediction should have killed the movement, but it didn't. Some of the followers of Miller began to reread the prophecies and they soon came up with an ingenious explanation. Miller had based his calculations on a passage in Daniel that spoke of the cleansing of the sanctuary. Now the explanation emerged that this cleansing had not taken place on earth but in heaven. On October 22, 1844, Jesus had entered the sanctuary in heaven and had begun to examine the records of all human beings who were living or had ever lived.

By means of this change in emphasis some of the followers of Miller were able to continue their intense interest in the prophecies and to proclaim the imminent return of Christ. For obviously if He had begun the examination of all records it was only a matter of time before the work would be completed and the end would take place. Several groups were organized into separate churches, and the largest of these is the Seventh-Day Adventist Church.

With such a start it isn't hard to understand that Seventh-Day Adventists concentrate much of their attention on the future. Of course, most Christian churches believe in the physical return of Christ. But the Adventists feel sure that the return will be very soon, though they have never made Miller's mistake of setting a date.

A great deal of the church's attention is focused on the prophecies in Daniel and Revelation. Very strange and literal fulfillments are worked out for many figurative passages of the Bible. Thus the whole history of the Roman Empire is made to fit these prophecies and obscure historical figures are brought forth to demonstrate the truth of their system.

Along with the fulfillment of prophecy go some other ideas about the future. According to the church's teaching, the soul does not go to heaven at death but "sleeps." Then when Jesus returns all true believers will be resurrected and taken to heaven for 1000 years. During this time the earth will remain an uninhabited wilderness. After the 1000 years Christ will return, resurrect the wicked, judge them and then destroy them. There is no eternal hell in Seventh-Day Adventist doctrine. As for the saved, they will spend eternity on a purified and cleansed earth.

While most Christians are not as concerned as they should be about the future, Seventh-Day Adventists find great strength in this direction. Stirred by the prospect of the immediate return of Christ, the church is zealous in its missionary activity and has spread into many foreign countries. While we do not share their interpretations of prophecy, we can learn something about zealous work from these people.

STATISTICS

```
Membership ......................... 350,000
Congregations ........................ 3,500
Clergy ............................... 3,100
```

TABLE OF COMPARISON

ADVENTISTS	LUTHERANS

TEACHINGS

ADVENTISTS	LUTHERANS
1. Accept the Trinity and the Atonement of Christ.	1. Same.
2. Accept Bible as Word of God but believe in the continuing spirit of prophecy.	2. Accept the Bible as Word of God.
3. Practice Baptism, Holy Communion and footwashing.	3. Practice Baptism and Holy Communion.
4. Regard observance of Saturday as binding for all times.	4. Saturday binding only for O.T. times.
5. Reject the existence of Hell.	5. Believe in the existence of hell.
6. Consider tithing and dietary rules binding on Christians.	6. Stress the liberty of the Christian under the gospel.

TYPE OF WORSHIP

Unliturgical.	Liturgical.

GOVERNMENT

Local churches have considerable power but a type of representative government is set up for business of church.	Congregational form of government in North America but power delegated to elected officials for some church work.

CHARACTERISTICS

Tend toward legalistic religion. Very zealous in missionary activity.	Not legalistic. Carry on program of missionary work also, but proportionately less active.

But this is a church that looks BOTH *ways,* and the other half of Seventh-Day Adventist teaching is directed toward the past. No church has been as anxious as this one to bring back into Christianity some of the customs and rules of the Old Testament. It is strange to find this blending of past and future in the same church.

The most obvious sign of this move toward the Old Testament is in the insistence on keeping Saturday rather than Sunday as a day of worship. This is where the denomination gets the "Seventh-Day" part of its name. This idea is not unique with Seventh-Day Adventists of course. There have always been some in the church who have criticized the shift from Saturday to Sunday for worship. In the last century a group of Baptists began to preach that Christians should go back to the Old Testament practice of observing a period from Friday at 6 p.m. to Saturday at 6 p.m. (the Jewish Sabbath) as the time for worship.

The Adventists put this idea into their teaching as their second major emphasis. One of the early leaders, a Mrs. Ellen White, claimed to have had a vision in which she saw Jesus in heaven displaying the Ten Commandments. A special halo surrounded the one that commands the keeping of the Sabbath Day.

This stress on the Sabbath has created no end of difficulty for the church, but it has also made the members determined to maintain their teachings. It might seem to make little difference what day a man keeps, but in our modern world it is confusing and disruptive to have a division on this issue. Seventh-Day Adventists have often had to surrender jobs because of their teachings, but many have endured this rather than work on what they consider the Lord's Day.

This looking to the past includes more than the Old Testament Sabbath. The stress on law, so characteristic of religion before Christ came, is restored in this church. Thus every member is commanded to tithe. In addition, dietary rules are observed, including the demand that the believer be a vegetarian. Seventh-Day Adventists are also forbidden to go to the theater, to play cards or to dance. They cannot smoke or use alcohol.

This emphasis on strict care of the body has had a strange and beneficial effect. The church has placed great stress on the art of healing and thus has established hospitals and sent out many medical missionaries. Indeed this has been one of its most fertile fields for the winning of converts.

The position of Mrs. Ellen White in the teaching of the church also needs some explanation. Seventh-Day Adventists are insistent that they base all their teachings on the Bible; they insist on a literal interpretation of almost every statement of Scripture. However, Mrs. White, one of the early leaders of the church, wrote a number of explanations of Christian truth that are accepted as containing divinely inspired material. She had "the spirit of prophecy," according to the teachings of the church, and her writings are widely circulated among Seventh-Day Adventists.

Lutherans put a great deal of stress on Christian education and the importance of the printed word. The Seventh-Day Adventists are also active in these fields. They have developed a school system that includes parochial schools as well as universities. They print literature in about 180 languages and conduct services in more than 600 tongues.

It's strange but true that any group which emphasizes some peculiar doctrine has a tendency to place all the emphasis at that point. Anyone who reads the teachings of the Adventists finds many teachings that are orthodox and acceptable to most Christians. The church believes in the Trinity, in the atonement of Christ, in religious liberty, and in salvation by faith.

Yet the major stress is revealed in the name of the church —Seventh-Day Adventists. Making the keeping of Saturday a necessity tends to nullify some of the emphasis on God's grace. The undue concern for the prophetic passages of the Bible constantly runs the risk that the plainer and more central truths are neglected.

No Lutheran would want to surrender the liberty of the gospel for the emphasis on a certain day of worship or any other rules. Nevertheless, we can learn zeal, liberality in giving and the need to prepare our hearts for Christ's return from these spiritual descendents of William Miller, the man who set the date for the end of the world.

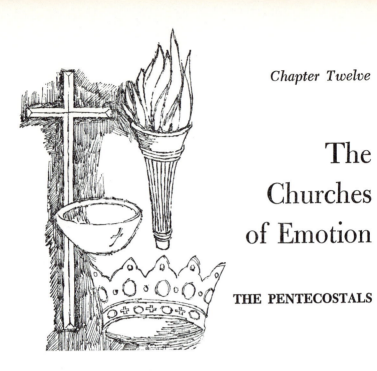

Chapter Twelve

The
Churches
of Emotion

THE PENTECOSTALS

Have you ever attended a service where the worship seemed lifeless, the hymns were sung without feeling, the liturgy conducted without interest, the sermon preached without conviction? If you've had such an experience, you know the importance of emotion in religion. Where there is no spark, no fire, the result is dull and depressing.

The only question is—how much emotion? Is God worshiped most effectively by dignity and solemnity or by intensity that shakes and stirs a man's whole nature? The Pentecostals, though they may differ among themselves in many ways, are all agreed that intensity (even if it borders on frenzy) is the best way. These people are the so-called "Holy Rollers," who shout God's praises until the wee small hours of the morning and who talk in tongues and may even roll on the floor in their ecstasy.

Most Lutherans would find Pentecostal worship a shocking contrast to our dignified liturgy. I once heard a group of these people praying. Each man prayed his own prayer as loud as he could, and the minister managed to outshout the rest. It seemed sheer bedlam; yet no one could doubt the sincerity or earnestness of the worshipers.

So let's take a closer look at this religion of emotion before we dismiss it as noise and nothing more. What began the Pentecostal movement, what does it teach, and how effective is it?

1. ORIGIN. The roots of Pentecostalism are found in the New Testament itself. When the Church began to grow, it was given certain outward signs to guide and help those first preachers. Thus there were remarkable miracles of healing performed at times by the apostles and others. In addition certain signs, such as speaking in tongues and prophesying, were present, especially when a new group was to be included in the church.

Thus when the Samaritans were first converted, the Holy Spirit came on them in a visible way. Similarly, when the Gentile Cornelius was to be baptized an external sign was given so that none could deny Cornelius' right to become a part of the church. Such signs continued for a time in the church, but then apparently the need for them ceased.

However, there have always been people in the church who have lamented this loss of miracle-working power and have tried to revive it among Christians. Modern Pentecostalism is just the latest in a long series of movements which have sought to revive the apostolic practices. And whenever the church grows cold and unemotional the

STATISTICS

Membership 900,000
Congregations 13,000
Clergy 15,000

TABLE OF COMPARISON

PENTECOSTALS   LUTHERANS

TEACHINGS

PENTECOSTALS	LUTHERANS
1. Regard the Bible as the inspired Word of God.	1. Same.
2. Believe in Trinity and in the divinity of Christ.	2. Same.
3. Usually two sacraments, sometimes footwashing added.	3. Two sacraments, baptism and Holy Communion.
4. Believe in a special baptism by the Holy Spirit, accompanied by speaking in tongues and other signs.	4. Believe the Holy Spirit given in Baptism. Tongues considered special New Testament signs.
5. Believe in Christ as a healer of all bodily as well as spiritual ills.	5. Bodily healing viewed as usually taking place through normal medical care.

TYPE OF WORSHIP

Highly emotional in hymns, prayers, and preaching. No form of worship. Great pressure put on hearers.	Liturgical worship. Service orderly and quiet. Can become formalism if worshiper isn't careful.

GOVERNMENT

Each congregation is highly independent but there are associations of congregations for common purposes.	Congregational government in America but some power surrendered to synods for common purposes.

CHARACTERISTICS

Has strongest appeal to those who seek emotional release in religion. Very successful among poorly educated.	Strongest appeal to middle class, although not exclusively so.

cry for the old-time fervor is heard among some sincere and well-meaning believers.

It's difficult to say just when this recent emphasis came into the church again to produce Pentecostalism. Some date the beginning from a revival in eastern Tennessee and western North Carolina in 1886. Others find the start in a movement among the students at Bethel Bible College, Topeka, Kansas, in 1901, where a revival produced the speaking in tongues and other Pentecostal signs. This movement spread to a Methodist church in Los Angeles and from there Pentecostalism appeared among many Bible-centered groups.

The first movement to form some kind of denomination took place at Hot Springs, Arkansas, in 1914, when the Assemblies of God was formed. This is still the largest of the groups under the Pentecostal banner, but there are scores of churches and independent groups in existence. Obviously the movement is very new and quite disorganized, but the churches continue to grow and spread out to new areas.

2. TEACHINGS. Because the movement is new and is often the product of individual leaders, Pentecostal churches exhibit many differences in doctrinal matters. However, there are four general ideas around which the teachings are grouped. This is the "four-square gospel," made famous by Aimee Semple McPherson in the 1920s. Let's glance at each teaching:

a. Christ as Savior. Pentecostal churches are orthodox in their stress on the atonement of Christ. No Lutheran could find fault with their emphasis on sin, on the need for conversion or the necessity of Christ to offer Himself as a sacrifice for sin. Indeed the teachings of the church are strongly Bible-centered and, though we might critize the interpretation at times, we would not quarrel with the Bible-centered or Christ-centered nature of the church's teaching.

b. Christ as Sanctifier. Here the peculiar stress of Pentecostalism begins. Being converted is not enough, as far as the teachings of this group are concerned. Conversion, accepting Christ, saves a man—but God has promised additional blessings. The Holy Spirit will come upon the Christian and give him a special experience, which usually consists of speaking in tongues. This may not happen immediately and the believer must be patient.

However, since this special outpouring always happens in the group, the worship services are aimed at producing or calling down the Spirit. So emotional and sometimes jazzy hymns are sung. The prayers are poured out with great emotional fervor. The preaching is aimed at arousing the congregation and finally, when the emotion is at its height, some one may begin to speak strangely or to manifest that he has been overcome by the Spirit. This is the sought-for blessing, more precious than the mere conversion of the individual, and it leaves an indelible mark on a man's mind.

c. Christ as Healer. Faith-healing is a widely discussed subject these days, with Oral Roberts and others putting forth their claims in this area. Pentecostals insist that Christ not only died to heal our *souls* but also to heal our *bodies.* For some this means a complete refusal to seek any medical help in time of sickness; for others the position is not quite that extreme.

However, the insistence is made that if a man has faith enough he can be healed of any sickness. One of the preachers insists that it is just as easy to be healed of a cancer as to be forgiven your sins.

Once again the pressure is emotional. Healing services are periods of great emotional outpourings for these people and it would be a miracle if someone wasn't healed or supposedly healed under such stress. Sometimes, however, since the emphasis is on the faith of the person, this is a cruel experience. For if the healing does not take place, the assumption is that the person did not have sufficient faith. The chance for quacks and trickery is great in this area, although again no one should doubt the sincerity of most Pentecostal healing services.

d. Christ as Coming King. Pentecostals are firm believers in the physical return of Christ, and they believe He will return very soon. Indeed many of them regard the appearance of signs in the church, such as talking in tongues, healing, etc., as evidences that we have reached the place in history where the Lord is sure to return. This stress on the coming Lord gives an urgency to the message of the church, driving the group to work and sacrifice because the time is short. Most Christians share with the Pentecostals a belief in the return of Christ, but not all are willing to state positively that we are close to the end.

3. SUCCESS. There is nothing so hard to measure as the size of the Pentecostal movement. Some groups refuse to publish any statistics. Also there is no clear-cut division that determines who are Pentecostals, since other groups share some but not all of the above ideas. Yet

there is no doubt that Pentecostalism has been remarkably successful, not only in North America but more particularly in overseas work. The churches have spread throughout Latin America at a much faster rate than other Protestant groups. Perhaps a few reasons for this remarkable growth are worth listing.

a. They work harder. Let's admit it—the Pentecostals are in earnest about their faith. They work among the poorer classes of people who are often neglected by the older, larger denominations. They offer to such people a new way of life and a sense of importance in this life and in the promise of the world to come.

b. They are taught to witness for their faith. Pentecostals are not afraid to talk about their faith. They may make nuisances of themselves, they may seem like fanatics to many, yet the fact that a man is willing to say what Jesus Christ has done for him is impressive and convincing.

c. They present a positive approach. Much modern Christianity is wishy-washy. There is no argument about black and white for the Pentecostal. He *knows* he's right and he backs up that feeling by the emotional experience which he has had.

d. They offer emotional freedom. We all like to give vent to our emotions at times, to yell at a football game or get involved in a crowd action. Pentecostalism gives vent to this under the name of religion. While such experiences may be an emotional jag and may result in a letdown afterward, this doesn't change the fact that at the time the person is caught up in a fervent experience.

Despite all this, Lutherans would say that emotion is

not the answer to every problem. Pentecostalism has real dangers, and those who fall away from the movement are terribly difficult to reach for the church ever again. Nevertheless, we can learn from these people too. We need more fervor in our singing and worship, a more positive attitude in our faith, and above all a greater willingness to witness to others about what our Lord has done for us.

Chapter Thirteen

Holiness and Healing

CHURCHES OF GOD

Recently, Lutheran groups in America have been having difficulties with their names. There simply don't seem to be enough distinctive names to satisfy the various branches or general bodies. And when all the re-naming has been done, many Lutherans are still going to be confused by the results.

But if *our* problems seem confusing, consider the *Church of God*. There are at least 200 independent bodies that incorporate these words in their title. Five groups, all claiming to be "The Church of God," have their separate headquarters at Cleveland, Tennessee. How would you like to distinguish among "The Church of God, M. A. Tomlinson, Overseer," "The Church of God, Homer A. Tomlinson, Overseer," "The Church of God, H. L. Chesser, Overseer," "The (Original) Church of God," "The Church of God, Inc.," etc.?

Another "Church of God" is identified by "Anderson, Indiana," its headquarters city; it began around 1881, earlier

100

than the Tennessee groups, as a restoration movement within existing churches. This branch is more conservative than the others, placing its major stress on Christian unity and personal holiness. It resembles the old-time Methodist church in doctrine and worship.

Fortunately there is enough family resemblance among these groups that we can get a general picture without too much trouble. All these churches are "Holiness" churches. This means that they have adopted a rather novel solution to one of the great problems in the Christian faith—the persistence of sin after one becomes a believer.

It must be admitted that this problem of sin is a difficult one. After a person comes to believe in Christ, he would like to do the Lord's will perfectly. But most Christians have found that it doesn't work that way—sin still remains and must be resisted day by day. This is what Luther means when he talks about dying daily to sin and rising to righteousness.

The "Holiness" groups have a different solution. They believe that after a person has become a believer, God will give him a second blessing so that he will become perfect. This is instantaneous, just as conversion is, and is to be sought with prayer and emotionalism. So, members of the Church of God who have received this experience insist that they are now sinless. They may be tempted by external things but there is no sin left in their souls.

How is it possible for people to convince themselves that they have reached perfection? Isn't this simply dishonesty? Part of the answer lies in the emotional atmosphere in which the members live. Church services or prayer meetings are held almost nightly and often last until the early hours

STATISTICS

Membership 400,000
Churches 9,000
Clergy 8,000

TABLE OF COMPARISON

CHURCH OF GOD	LUTHERANS
TEACHINGS	
1. The Bible is the Word of God.	1. Same.
2. Man is justified by faith in Christ's work.	2. Same.
3. Man can then become perfect by a special gift of the Holy Spirit.	3. Christian life is a growth toward perfection, never completed in this life.
4. Man can receive a special baptism of the Holy Spirit to "talk in tongues."	4. The Holy Spirit is given in baptism. "Tongues" considered special New Testament signs.
5. Three sacraments — baptism, holy communion, footwashing.	5. Two sacraments—baptism and holy communion.
TYPE OF WORSHIP	
No set form. Worship highly emotional and often in humble surroundings and temporary quarters.	Liturgical worship. Service orderly and quiet. Usually seek permanent and attractive churches.
GOVERNMENT	
Some branches under control of an overseer who appoints pastors. Three kinds of clergy: ministers of the gospel, evangelists, exhorters.	Congregational government in America with some power delegated to elected boards for common work.
CHARACTERISTICS	
Greatest strength in the South and in foreign lands. Clergy usually not highly educated.	High standard for clerical training. General appeal to middle class.

of the morning. Bible reading and intense witnessing are encouraged. Consequently, when the member contrasts what he was before being sanctified and what he has become, it's easy to feel that perfection has arrived.

It's like a student who has been getting a grade of around 20 on his test papers—and then by constant study manages to raise his grade to 75. He is so elated that he is likely to forget what remains to be done. And no one will deny that many people under the influence of the holiness movement *are* much better people than they were before.

In addition, certain outward standards are set by the Church of God and the believer tends to identify these standards with holiness. Church of God members are forbidden to use tobacco or alcohol, to wear ornaments or cosmetics, to attend movies. Members are required to be tithers, and Bible reading plus prayer are constantly encouraged as evidences of holiness. Thus the things people do can make them think they actually are "perfect."

However, much as we may admire the personal holiness demonstrated by some of these people, the idea of perfection is bound to produce two evils in the church. Some are tempted to become hypocritical and proud, refusing to see their own sins. Others are driven to despair when they find that what they thought was complete holiness isn't as perfect as they imagined, that subtle and internal sins remain. People who have had this experience are extremely difficult to get back into any Christian church.

Faith healing is also a part of the teachings of the Church of God. Most members refuse to go to a doctor for any type of sickness. Thus the wife of one of the church founders suffered terrible pains for a long time and refused all medical assistance even when friends threatened to get the police to interfere. Without debating the possibilities of faith healing, it is sad when people are denied the aid of modern medicine because of a belief that God will heal all sickness apart from medical knowledge.

The noisy type of worship which people have dubbed "Holy Rollers" is usually part of Church of God practices too. There is a desire to receive a special baptism from the Holy Spirit so that the members can talk in tongues. A. J. Tomlinson, one of the founders of the Church of God, tells of visions that he received, of people crying out for several hours in secret tongues, even of organists playing the organ while under the influence of the Spirit.

Such demonstrations do provide emotional outlets for the members and help increase the fervor of the believers. But there are some sad penalties paid at times for this. Tongues are interpreted to suit the desire of the interpreter. Children are often whipped into a frenzy that is dangerous for their emotional life. Some of the divisions in the Church of God family have come because men have taken advantage of these emotional scenes and have pushed their private interpretations.

It is not possible to understand the Church of God completely without knowing the story of A. J. Tomlinson, the founder of many of the groups. Indeed it is said that 44 church groups in America owe their origin to Tomlinson's work!

He was born in Indiana, although his family came from North Carolina and most of his success was won in the hills of Carolina and Tennessee. In 1896, while working as a seller of Bibles and religious literature, Tomlinson came in contact with the Pentecostal revivals being conducted by the Spurlings, father and son, in western North Carolina.

Tomlinson was profoundly moved by what he saw. The people in the area were poor, often illiterate, highly emotional and torn between religious longings and low moral standards. In the revivals being conducted by the Spurlings, moonshiners, thieves and others were being changed and caught up by the emotional fervor of the preaching.

It wasn't long before Tomlinson himself began to preach and to center his work at Cleveland, Tennessee. He carried on the typical Pentecostal type of service with emotional hymns, loud preaching, fervent prayers and often noisy shrieks from the congregation. In his diary he tells how it was not unusual for the services to continue until 2 a.m. In one year he preached 203 sermons and resolved to do better the next year.

Religion was no light matter in this section of the country. Sometimes the police were summoned to the meetings, particularly when irate neighbors objected to the noisy demonstrations. And gangs of toughs often tried to destroy the work. Sometimes they attacked the tent where Tomlinson was preaching, sometimes they stoned Tomlinson's house, and on one occasion three men fired 60 shots into a house in an effort to kill this preacher.

In addition there was constant trouble among Tomlinson's followers. Highly emotional gatherings can produce violent tempers. For a time Tomlinson and a rival faction had to share the church building, by court order. In 1922 Tomlinson was ousted from the very churches he had organized and forced to begin all over again. At his death in 1943 he had again built up a large following but it was split into three fragments with two of his sons each heading a segment.

Despite all this opposition, or perhaps because of it, the Church of God has continued to grow. Moreover it has made tremendous impacts in foreign lands, particularly in Central and South America. The fervor of the members, the willingness to worship without elaborate buildings and the lack of concern for an educated clergy has freed men and money for foreign mission work. It is strange but true that Protestantism in South America and Africa is more often represented by groups such as the Church of God than by the older, more sedate denominations.

If there is one lesson we need to learn from the Church of God it is this—no section of the population should be neglected by our gospel. The Church of God moved into an area that was served rather gingerly by the larger denominations. It reached people that others were inclined to call "trash." And although we may not like some of the methods used, we must admit that the Gospel has been preached fervently to people who were formerly passed by or neglected by other groups.

Jesus didn't put any limitation on the Gospel. The minute we do, someone will move in and reach the neglected ones. The Church of God is doing this very thing. Perhaps we can take a leaf from their book and make sure that we are reaching all who need Christ's saving message.

Chapter Fourteen

The Church
That Refuses
to Be One

JEHOVAH'S
WITNESSES

Few people reading these words will be totally ignorant of the group known as Jehovah's Witnesses. Perhaps you have met them on the street corner offering for sale their religious publications. Perhaps they have knocked at your door and almost pushed their way in to urge you to hear a recorded talk. Perhaps you have heard their messages blared at you from a sound truck.

Or you may have read about the Witnesses in the newspaper. They have a remarkable talent for getting into the spotlight by getting into trouble. Young men of the group refuse to serve in the armed forces and this stirs up controversy. Children are taught to refuse to salute the flag or to sing patriotic songs, which is sure to provoke comment. Members of the sect also refuse to receive blood transfusions, even if their lives are in danger, and this also gets considerable publicity.

Who are these people whose teachings seem so strange and fanatical to most Christians? Where did they come from? According to their own account they have been in existence from the beginning of time. Abel is called the first Jehovah's Witness. Actually they had their beginning about 75 years ago in the work and teachings of Charles Taze Russell.

Russell was a layman in Pittsburgh who gathered a group of young men around him for Bible study. He had two ideas in mind: to find an explanation for hell and to study the prophetic books of the Bible, particularly *Daniel* and *Revelation.* Russell's group expanded so rapidly that by 1878 he became pastor of an independent congregation. The next year he began publishing a magazine known as *The Watchtower.*

Russell was a prolific writer. Books, pamphlets, magazines poured forth from his pen. Between 1886 and 1904 he published a six-volume study of the Bible which sold more than 15 million copies before Russell's death in 1916. Despite their leader's involvement in a bitter divorce suit and other court entanglements, Russell's followers grew in numbers and in zeal.

Russell was followed by Judge Rutherford as leader of the group. Rutherford had a keen legal mind and a remarkable ability as orator and organizer. He too was a voluminous writer and soon his publications eclipsed those of his predecessor. It was under Rutherford's leadership that the group adopted the name "Jehovah's Witnesses," taking this title from Isaiah 43:10: "Ye are my witnesses." Previously such names as Russellites, Millennial Dawnists and International Bible Students had been used. At Rutherford's death in 1942 the movement passed under the con-

trol of Nathan Homer Knorr, but it now seems to be run
by a committee.

So far there is nothing new in this. Many groups owe
their origin to the leadership of a gifted Bible teacher or
an energetic leader. Usually such groups either wither
away or settle down to the general routine of a Christian
denomination. What makes Jehovah's Witnesses unique?
What do they teach that sets them apart from other religious
groups?

In the first place, Jehovah's Witnesses insist that they
aren't a church at all. Indeed, they attack all organized
religion as a device of the devil and are especially vehement
in their assaults on Roman Catholicism. They meet, not
in churches, but in "kingdom halls." They have no ordained ministry, for each member of the group considers
himself a minister. It is this teaching that has caused so
much trouble with draft boards since all Witnesses demand
to be classified as ministers and thus draft exempt.

The teachings of this group employ many of the terms
used by orthodox Christians, but their understanding of
the terms is far from the normal one. Thus Jesus is called
"Son of God" and yet the doctrine of the Trinity is denied.
Supposedly Jesus was once the Archangel Michael; then
He became a man (but nothing more) while here on earth.
Now He is in heaven but He was not resurrected; His *body*
either was taken to heaven or it seemingly evaporated.

Jehovah's Witnesses also talk about the Atonement, but
they don't mean that Christ paid the penalty for our sins.
Rather, by His death Jesus made it possible for every man
to have a second chance to believe. There is no hell in

```
┌──────────────────────────────────────────────┐
│               STATISTICS                       │
│  Membership (est.) ..................... 250,000 │
│  Churches .............................   4,000 │
│  Clergy ...............................         │
└──────────────────────────────────────────────┘
```

TABLE OF COMPARISON

JEHOVAH'S WITNESSES   LUTHERANS

TEACHINGS

JEHOVAH'S WITNESSES	LUTHERANS
1. Reject the Trinity. Only Jehovah is God.	1. Accept the Trinity — Father, Son and Holy Spirit.
2. Reject the Divinity of Christ. Consider Him a created being.	2. Accept the Divinity of Christ, the Son of God from all eternity.
3. Believe in a second chance for all men.	3. Believe that eternal welfare of all is determined in this life.
4. Reject the idea of hell. Evil souls are simply annihilated.	4. Accept the reality of hell as taught by the Scriptures.

TYPE OF WORSHIP

JEHOVAH'S WITNESSES	LUTHERANS
No liturgy. Services largely Bible study and sermons. No Sunday school.	A formal liturgical worship. Seek to train through Sunday school and other educational programs.

GOVERNMENT

JEHOVAH'S WITNESSES	LUTHERANS
Ruled by a president and various sectional leaders. No ordained ministers.	Congregational form of government in America. An ordained ministry.

CHARACTERISTICS

JEHOVAH'S WITNESSES	LUTHERANS
Zealous and fanatical, believing that they alone have the truth.	Believe that wherever Christ is confessed as Lord and Savior, Christians can be found.
Baptism by immersion. Communion once a year but received by only a few.	No stress on the mode of baptism. Communion offered frequently for all believers.

their teachings; those who reject the second chance are simply annihilated.

At first glance it would seem that no religious group is more devoted to the Bible itself. Indeed, some of the books published are more than half Biblical quotations. But the use is peculiar. Scripture passages are twisted and lifted out of place. Thus Genesis 9:4, which prohibits the eating of meat with the blood in it, is used to prove that blood transfusions are wrong. Jeremiah 10:3, which deals with the making of idols from wood, is employed to show that Christmas trees are wrong. The three friends of Job are said to represent the three allies of Satan, the religious, the political and the commercial powers of the world.

No wonder some people say, "You can prove anything from the Bible." You can, if it's used in this fashion.

The chief teachings of Jehovah's Witnesses center around the prophetic passages of the Bible. Thus earth's history is divided into three periods: from creation to the flood the earth was ruled by angels; from the flood to 1914 Satan was the ruler; from 1914 on, Christ has been the ruler. At present Christ is gathering a select group of 144,000 who are to rule with Him in heaven. When this group is gathered, there will come a terrible battle, Armageddon, at which time Satan's forces will be destroyed and this world will be ruled by some of the great leaders from the Old Testament.

During this millennium, the earth will become perfect again. All the dead are to be raised and given a second chance to believe. At the end of the 1000 years Satan is released and again deceives some men. Finally Satan and all his followers are destroyed and eternal life begins in earnest. Christ and the select ones will reign in heaven; the rest of mankind will be on this earth. This will be the theocracy, the true rule of Jehovah over His creation.

With such a system of faith it isn't hard to see how Jehovah's Witnesses get into trouble with governments and churches alike. For the Witnesses refuse to have anything to do with earthly governments; they feel themselves a part of Jehovah's kingdom alone. And they insist that all religion except their own is a racket, a creation of Satan. Indeed, they are so completely separated from all other churches that they now have their own version of the Bible to back up some of their ideas.

One can't help wondering how people get involved in such a strange variation and contradiction of orthodox Christianity. Many people who once were faithful church members now are the most zealous in condemning the church and in exalting the teachings of Russell and Rutherford. How does it happen?

First we must recognize the value of being positive in religion. The Witnesses are *sure*. They have an answer for *every* question. In contrast, some Christian groups today are wishy-washy in their beliefs, not really standing by the teachings of the Bible. You can't beat something with nothing, and the assurance of the Witnesses is convincing to many people.

Moreover, Jehovah's Witnesses are experts at exploiting every weakness in the church. There are many people today who do feel that religion is a racket and sometimes the church has helped foster such a viewpoint by losing sight of the real goal of Christianity. The attacks of the Witnesses are bitter and hard to take but perhaps the church needs this as a judgment on its own errors and weaknesses.

No one should discount the power of zeal either. The early Christians swept all before them because they believed what they taught and were willing to suffer and sacrifice for their church. The Jehovah's Witnesses have captured some of this spirit, but without also retaining the teachings of the early church. It takes zeal to stand on a street corner and sell church publications. It takes nerve to go from house to house as a witness to the faith. Much as we decry some of the false teachings, we should not overlook the fanatical devotion of these people. We could use some of this zeal in the church today.

One of the remarkable causes for success of Jehovah's Witnesses is their use of printed material. If ever there was a religion established by the power of the printing press, this is it. The church has become eminently successful in the production of cheap but effective propaganda. The publications are sold, or given away if necessary, but the material reaches people. Over 300,000,000 copies of the writings of Judge Rutherford were distributed before his death.

No one would class Jehovah's Witnesses as an orthodox Christian denomination. They represent an offshoot of the Christian witness, a scourge for the weaknesses of other groups, including our own Lutheran Church. Perhaps from them we can learn where we have fallen short in spreading the truth of God's Word. The "church" that refuses to be one can make the Church more conscious of its great task in the world.

Chapter Fifteen

Religion Made Easy

CHRISTIAN SCIENTISTS

Who are more religious, men or women? Most people would say "women"—and a look at the average church on Sunday morning would seem to confirm that view. Women usually outnumber men at the services and generally take a more active part in church work.

Yet few women have had any part in establishing or developing the leading denominations and religious societies.

There is one notable exception—Christian Science. This group, included in our series because it claims the name "Christian," was founded by Mary Baker Eddy. And so firmly did she put her imprint on the group that in the 50 years since her death no other leader of any importance has arisen among Christian Scientists.

What kind of person was Mary Baker Eddy? To the followers of this religion, she was a divinely inspired woman who wrote a book, *Science and Health with a Key to the Scriptures,* that is virtually on a plane with the Bible. For those opposed to Mrs. Eddy, she was a nervous, neurotic woman, illogical and poorly educated, who stole most of her ideas from others.

But the nature of Mrs. Eddy's character isn't too important. The thing that can not be forgotten is the remarkable success of this controversial woman. At the age of 50 she was a complete failure, almost penniless and friendless. Yet when she died at 89, she numbered her followers in the thousands and had established a strong, wealthy church organization. How could one frail woman accomplish so much?

At this point there is violent disagreement. To the believers in her teaching, Mary Baker Eddy discovered the real secret of the Bible and of the teachings of Jesus. She is really the "Comforter" whom Jesus speaks about, for she brought men to an understanding of Divine Science. So Christian Scientists believe that their religion is clear, logical and easy to grasp.

Those who oppose Christian Science get just the opposite reaction. They find it a religion of almost unbelievable contradictions, a study in nonsense. They point out that the book written by Mrs. Eddy is monotonous and repetitious. They believe she is neither logical nor clear in her statements.

Actually the clue to Christian Science does not lie in its clarity or lack of clarity. The thing that dare not be overlooked is that Mrs. Eddy found a clever way to deal with most of the problems of Christianity. She seized on the simplest, easiest answer to each difficulty, whether it was logical or not. At the same time she continued to employ the language of orthodox Christianity, even when she gave words an entirely different meaning.

```
┌─────────────────────────────────────────────────┐
│                 STATISTICS                        │
│  Membership (est.) ..................... 500,000  │
│  Congregations ....................... ......     │
│  Clergy ............................. none        │
└─────────────────────────────────────────────────┘
```

TABLE OF COMPARISON

CHRISTIAN SCIENTISTS	LUTHERANS

TEACHINGS

CHRISTIAN SCIENTISTS	LUTHERANS
1. Accept the Bible, but as interpreted by Mrs. Eddy's book, "Science and Health with the Key to the Scriptures."	1. Accept the Bible as inspired Word of God.
2. Reject the Triune nature of God.	2. Believe in the Triune nature of God.
3. Believe sin, sickness and death are only illusions of the mind.	3. Believe in the reality of sin. Sickness and death are a result of man's sin.
4. Deny the reality of matter.	4. Believe in the reality of God's Creation.

TYPE OF WORSHIP

CHRISTIAN SCIENTISTS	LUTHERANS
Hymns and selections read from the Bible and Mrs. Eddy's book by two readers. No real observance of the sacraments and no ordained ministry.	A liturgical form of worship used, led by an ordained minister. A sermon usually preached. Sacraments observed as commanded by Christ with actual elements of water, bread and wine.

GOVERNMENT

CHRISTIAN SCIENTISTS	LUTHERANS
Rigid control by mother church in Boston	No set form of government but in America the congregational form followed.

CHARACTERISTICS

CHRISTIAN SCIENTISTS	LUTHERANS
Strong stress on healing. Powerful appeal to those seeking an easy answer to religious problems.	Strong stress on salvation through faith. Not much emphasis on physical healing.

One of the puzzling problems of our faith is the doctrine of the Trinity. Men have wrestled with the idea of three Persons in one Godhead for centuries. Mrs. Eddy solved it with the greatest of ease. She made the Holy Spirit simply a characteristic of God, and denied the essential deity of Jesus Christ. At the same time she continued to speak of God as Life, Truth and Love, a trinity in unity. Thus Christian Scientists can eat their cake and have it too. There is no mystery for them about God's nature but if anyone wants to talk about the Trinity, they will still use the term.

The presence of sin is also a troubling question for a believer. How can there be sin in a world made by a good God? Are we born in sin? How can we get rid of it? Once again Mrs. Eddy came up with a clever answer. She simply denied that evil exists. If God is good and God is all, then there can't *be* any evil. Man, created in the image of God, cannot have evil in his nature. So evil is simply an error of the mind. To banish evil from your world, all you have to do is convince yourself that it doesn't exist.

Such a brazen denial of reality almost takes your breath away. In a world filled with sin, it seems unbelievable that anyone would deny that evil exists. Yet once you get over the shock, you see the cleverness of such a view. "Forgiveness of sin" means you become convinced that you have no sin. The atonement of Christ means that Christ shows you how to banish the idea of sin from your mind. Jesus is not a divine savior but the Way-shower. Once again the orthodox terms are employed but the meaning is entirely different.

Another disturbing problem for Christians is the existence

of sickness in the world. How can a good God permit sickness to come upon His children on this earth? The Book of Job wrestles with this difficulty and finally decides that such matters must be left with God.

Once again Mrs. Eddy finds the easy solution. She simply denies that sickness exists, and while she's at it she denies the existence of matter itself. Such things are all in the mind. So, healing takes place when an individual becomes convinced that he isn't sick (there isn't any such thing as sickness).

This was a masterstroke on the part of the clever Mrs. Eddy. She claimed that she was healed instantaneously in 1866 after being injured in a skating accident and from this point on she taught that there was no real sickness in the world. The gains for Christian Science are enormous at this point. There *are* many people in the world who suffer from imaginary ills and Christian Science convinces such people that they can be healed. Moreover, anyone who *isn't* healed is simply informed he doesn't yet have enough faith to believe that sickness is imaginary.

*This same pattern—the easy solution—*is repeated over and over in Christian Science. The controversies that have arisen among Christians over the sacraments are avoided by simply abolishing the sacraments and substituting mental concentration on the benefits promised.

Problems arising from a trained ministry are avoided by abolishing the office of the ministry and substituting two readers at each service who read from the Bible and from *Science and Health*. At every step Mrs. Eddy found a solution, an easy one, for the difficulties of the church.

Anyone who looks at Christian Science is first moved

to wonder how people can be led to accept such teachings as those of Mrs. Eddy. How can people be taught to believe that there is no sin, no sickness, no reality in matter? What quirk in human nature gives appeal to Christian Science?

The answer isn't hard to find. The simple, easy picture of life which forms the basis of this religion appeals to many people. It is pleasant to think that there is no sin. It's nice, although not always convincing, to claim that you aren't sick even when you feel that you are. Moreover, such teachings ask no sacrifice on your part to help others who are sick or miserable since their troubles are all in their minds anyway.

Mrs. Eddy's clever use of Christian terminology is also a means of bringing people into her church. While Christian Science is not considered a Christian church, there are undoubtedly some people in the group who are deceived into thinking that such terms as God, Trinity, Sin, Atonement, etc., retain the normal Christian meaning.

But perhaps the greatest appeal exerted is that of healing. While Christian Scientists insist that healing is only a part of their faith, the majority of those in the church have probably been drawn by this emphasis. The midweek services feature testimonials from those who have been healed, and this arouses interest in the hearts of many afflicted people. Mrs. Eddy hit upon a sound principle in her stress on the importance of the mind in healing, and this has become a powerful means of reaching many.

It must not be forgotten either that this religion makes good use of the printed and spoken word. Free lectures are given by specially trained lecturers from the mother church in Boston. Free literature is distributed in bus and railway stations. One of the finest daily papers in America, the *Christian Science Monitor,* is sponsored by the church. Public reading rooms are attached to each church and are also often sponsored in a prominent, downtown place in a big city.

Nor can it be denied that the Church of Christ, Scientist (to use its official name) is wonderfully organized. It is run with amazing efficiency. All church life revolves around the mother church in Boston and every member of the branch churches pays annual dues to the mother church. Thus there is complete control over the membership; if someone gets out of line his dues are simply refused and he has no standing in the church. All lectures are prepared under the direction of the church. The practitioners who heal are trained and licensed by the controlling board. Only the Bible and Mrs. Eddy's words are heard in the church services. It is an efficient control system.

Much as we may marvel at such features, we cannot think of Christian Science except as a warning to the unwary Christian. Here are words that mislead rather than guide. Here is religion made easy.

Chapter Sixteen

The Reasonable Church

THE UNITARIAN-UNIVERSALISTS

Did you ever try to argue religion with someone who was not a believer? It can be a most distressing experience. For many of the teachings of the Christian Church are not subject to logical reasoning or proof.

Try to establish by logic that there are three Persons in the Godhead or that God forgives sins or that the sacraments bring special blessings. Unless your opponent is a little weak in the head, you're probably outmaneuvered at every turn.

The truth is that certain Christian teachings are known only through God's revelation. They are not subject to proof but must be accepted by faith. This doesn't mean these truths are nonsensical; it does mean there's a limit to man's reasoning ability. Although Christian groups have differed as to the content of our faith, few have denied that some truths must be simply believed and are not subject to man's reasoning faculties.

One religious group having Christian origins, however, does refuse to accept anything which cannot be proved by reason. The Unitarian denomination, a small but rather influential group, has from its beginning insisted on *reason* as the only criterion for the measure of truth. Nothing which cannot be proved by logic or evidence is acceptable to the Unitarians. (The latest statement of Unitarian teaching refuses even to identify the group as "Christian," which Unitarians for a long time claimed to be.)

It isn't hard to see what happens to Christian doctrine when approached from this viewpoint. Obviously the doctrine of the Trinity is the first victim of man's reason. Indeed, it was the rejection of the triune nature of God which gave the Unitarians their name (not *trini*-tarian but *uni*-tarian). They demoted Jesus to the stature of a man and considered the Holy Spirit as merely another name or manifestation of God.

As indicated, the divinity of Christ is also a casualty. While at first Unitarians accepted many of the miracles of Jesus and gave Him a position close to the Father, today He is regarded as a great man who possessed remarkable religious insight. He was divine only in the sense that each of us is divine or has a divine spark within him.

The grace of God and the forgiveness of sins also are eliminated when reason is the only judge. Unitarians believe in a do-it-yourself type of religion. They do not deny that there is sin or weakness in man's natural self, but man has the capacity to improve himself, they believe. The goal of religion then is to help man make himself a credit to God and to society. So salvation is by character, not by grace.

The Bible too occupies a different place in this church which is guided by reason. The Scriptures are not God's Word but a record of man's religious longings and growth. Unitarians reverence the Bible but they hold in equally high esteem other religious writings, including the sacred books of other religions. Nothing is gained in a discussion with a Unitarian by insisting that a certain truth is taught in the Bible, for he may simply insist that man now has more light on that particular subject.

Perhaps a few more examples will show how radically historic Christian teaching is changed by Unitarians. The Virgin Birth of Jesus becomes a poetic legend. Christmas is the victory of light over darkness. Easter is a symbol of the immortality of the soul. The atonement of Christ is regarded as a doctrine which insults God. And so it goes.

It isn't hard to see why orthodox denominations refuse to include the Unitarians among the Christian churches. Indeed modern Unitarians have ceased to regard themselves as such and proudly proclaim that they are a scientific and liberal 20th-century church. Recently they have united with the Universalist Church, a somewhat smaller denomination which arose in New England when some men insisted that there was no hell but that all men would ultimately be saved—"universal salvation." (The new body is named the Unitarian Universalist Association.)

We must not think that Unitarian teachings are all negative, despite the denial of most orthodox beliefs. Five

STATISTICS

Membership 200,000
Congregations 700
Clergy 600

TABLE OF COMPARISON

UNITARIANS   LUTHERANS

TEACHINGS

1. The Bible is an expression of purely human religious ideas and development.
2. No binding creed or doctrine.
Reason the only true guide.
3. The unity of God emphasized.
4. Jesus viewed as a good man, our
example.
5. Salvation by character.

1. The Bible is the revealed Word of
God.
2. Creeds express understanding of
Christian truth. Faith essential.
3. God's triune nature confessed.
4. Jesus both divine and human, our
Savior.
5. Salvation by grace through faith.

TYPE OF WORSHIP

An increasing use of historical liturgical forms. However, worship
viewed as a means to improve the
worshiper, not as an effort to glorify
God.

Liturgical worship. Prime objective is
to glorify God and to thank Him
for His many blessings.

GOVERNMENT

Completely congregational. Churches
are associated in a voluntary national group but retain independence.

Congregational government in America but some power delegated to
elected boards and officials.

CHARACTERISTICS

Appeal made to "liberal" and scientific man. Rather strong influence
among intellectuals. Reason is the
guiding light.

Appeal made to all groups, although
membership is largely middle class.
Faith made basis for appeal.

basic doctrines are stressed: 1. The fatherhood of God; 2. The brotherhood of man; 3. The perfectibility of man; 4. Salvation by character, not by grace; 5. The right to personal freedom of belief.

This last teaching may seem to deny all the others and in a sense it does. Unitarians have no creed which all must accept. They think of religion as a completely personal thing. Each man is to believe what seems reasonable to him and, if two differ in their opinions, that disturbs no one. While many churches have tried to boast that they have no creed, Unitarianism comes as close to that goal as possible, for there are no real standards of membership or of doctrine.

You may wonder how such a strange and peculiar form of Christianity came into existence. Actually there have been a number of unrelated efforts to start such churches in the history of Christendom. This is not strange for whenever man begins to elevate his own reason above the revelation of God's Word, some form of Unitarianism usually results.

American Unitarianism arose at the close of the 18th century, the so-called "Age of Reason." At first it was only a small movement in New England Congregationalism. As is usually the case when a new idea arises, there were bitter fights and divisions in the churches. For a time Unitarianism captured the major minds of New England and also managed to take over many of the historic churches in that area. At one time, 12 of the 14 Congregational Churches in Boston went over to this new "liberal" Christianity.

A number of famous preachers helped Unitarians to grow for a time. William Ellery Channing, a skillful orator, gave the first real statement of the new church's faith in

1819. Later the famous Theodore Parker held Boston crowds spellbound with his oratory and his learning. Ralph Waldo Emerson was a Unitarian preacher for several years and although he later gave up the pulpit, he continued to be an influential figure in Unitarianism.

But Unitarianism did not grow. It did not have the missionary zeal of other denominations. Its appeal was to the intellect. It was better able to win converts from other groups than to reach out as a missionary faith. It has been decreasing in proportional membership during the 20th century.

Yet this church which bases its teachings on reason is important in American church life, even though it has never been a large group. The appeal to the intellect has won Unitarians a great many famous men and women. Thus the church has had an influence far out of proportion to its numbers. Six presidents of the United States have been numbered among its adherents. Such men as Daniel Webster, Henry Wadsworth Longfellow and Horace Mann have also been Unitarians.

In addition, Unitarian teachings have had widespread influence in the more orthodox denominations. Indeed, it is the boast of this group that there are more Unitarians in the standard denominations than in the actual Unitarian organization itself. This is probably true. For Unitarianism appeals to man's pride of intellect. It requires no confession of sins, no admission of dependence on God's grace. It demands no adherence to any creed, no surrender of any personal viewpoint. Each man can be what he wants to be, the captain of his fate, the savior of his own soul.

Such ideas have found a response among many who still

cling to orthodox names and groups. We cannot help feel sad at those who cover their Unitarianism with the cloak of orthodoxy. The Unitarian Church is at least honest in its viewpoint. It may reject many of the teachings that we hold dear but it does not seek to deceive anyone at this point.

In fact, humanly speaking, we can be glad there is a Unitarian Church. For here, spelled out for all to see, is religion with faith and revelation fully removed. Here is what Christianity becomes when reason is made the ruler, rather than the servant, of the Bible. Here is what man's pride drives him to when he refuses to bow under God's Word.

Unitarianism began as a liberal point of view in Christianity. It sought at first only to make Christianity reasonable. But it ended by denying almost every precious Christian doctrine and finally has even disclaimed the name of Christian. Today it stands as a warning to those who would seek to make our faith a thing of the mind alone.

Chapter Seventeen

Some Other Churches

TEN SMALLER GROUPS

The parade of denominations is a long one. Indeed, men have written large descriptive books on the subject without managing to cover every religious group in America. Even if there were space to speak about every denomination, the list would be out of date in six months for churches are constantly splitting or combining, changing their names or modifying their doctrines.

Most of the smaller denominations are not represented in every section of the country. Perhaps you never have met a Moravian or a member of an Old Catholic church. Yet these smaller segments of the Church are important to those who love their teachings, and it is also true that some groups have made an impression on American church life far out of proportion to their numbers. So let's take a look at a few of the groups making up "the rest of the churches."

1. *The Evangelical United Brethren.* This is a fairly new church organization, founded in 1946, but it represents a merger of the *United Brethren in Christ* and *The Evangelical Church.* It was not too difficult for these two churches to unite, for both are the result of the Methodist revival coming into contact with German-speaking people in Pennsylvania.

Actually the Evangelical Church was intended to be a branch of Methodism but the German language proved to be a barrier. So Jacob Albright, a Lutheran who had become a Methodist preacher, set up his own organization in 1803 but kept Methodist doctrines and practices.

The United Brethren began under the leadership of Philip Otterbein and Martin Boehm, the former a Reformed preacher, the latter a Mennonite. But when a church was organized in 1800 the Methodist guidance was strong here too.

Today, many of the Methodist features still remain. The stress is on personal holiness and an experience of salvation rather than on doctrine. Worship is usually non-liturgical and the methods of baptism and holy communion are not fixed. Strangely enough, the EUB now has branches in Germany.

2. *The Reformed Church in America* (Dutch Reformed). Anyone who has read "Rip Van Winkle" or "The Legend

STATISTICS

Group	Churches	Members
Evangelical United Brethren	4300	750,000
Reformed (Dutch)	1500	460,000
Nazarenes	4400	300,000
Brethren	2300	280,000
Salvation Army	1300	250,000
Mennonites-Amish	1600	160,000
Friends (Quakers)	1000	125,000
Covenant-Ev. Free	900	100,000
Old Catholics	120	100,000
Moravians	200	70,000

of Sleepy Hollow" is aware that the Dutch were among the early settlers in America. They came for trade and commerce, not for religious freedom, but they did bring their Reformed teachings with them. The first Dutch Reformed Church in America was organized in 1628 in New Amsterdam.

Because the Dutch language was retained for a long time and because there weren't too many immigrants from the Netherlands, the church didn't grow too rapidly. Today it has centers of strength in Michigan and Iowa as well as New York.

Teachings and worship are similar to most churches that grew out of the Calvinistic reformation, though the Dutch Reformed have remained highly conservative. The Bible is considered of supreme authority. Baptism and Holy Communion are considered signs rather than means of grace. Admission to membership is by confession of faith before the pastors and elders of the church. This denomination is one of the few Protestant groups which believes firmly in Christian day schools.

3. *The Church of the Nazarene.* This church has come into existence by accumulation. Eight separate groups have become a part of the Church of the Nazarene, and several of these groups were the products of prior mergers. The basis of the fellowship in shown by a rather significant change of name: originally the church bore the name "Pentecostal" but this was dropped to avoid misconceptions. For the Nazarenes represent the moderate or "right wing" of the Pentecostal or Holiness groups.

The most distinctive doctrine is sanctification or holiness. The church stresses the old Methodist doctrine, revived by the Holiness groups, that the Holy Spirit will give perfection or holiness to an individual instantaneously. This was one of the distinctive teachings of the great revival movements and it is rekindled in the Nazarene Church. This stress on perfection is manifested in such things as abstaining from tobacco and the use of alcoholic beverages, etc.

However, the extreme position of many Pentecostal groups is not found among the Nazarenes. Thus they do not emphasize speaking in tongues; they accept baptism by sprinkling as well as by immersion; they do not refuse medical aid although they believe in divine healing.

The congregations once worshiped in store fronts almost exclusively, but today attractive houses of worship are being built. A group of members are growing up whose parents were members of the church. It remains to be seen whether the revived spirit of Wesley will settle down again to a less emotional type of church.

4. *The Church of the Brethren.* The Brethren, sometimes called Dunkers or Dunkards or German Baptists,
are noted for one distinctive doctrine—opposition to force
of any kind. They refuse to fight in a war, they refuse
to take an oath of allegiance, they refuse to go to court
in a legal matter. They even refuse to believe in infant
baptism because it involves, according to their interpretation, the use of force to baptize a child before it is old
enough to choose for itself.

Such views have involved the church in difficulty. Originally most of these people were German Lutherans, but
when they began to teach their strange doctrines, persecution broke out. In 1719 they began coming to America.
Here they have managed to live with a minimum of difficulty, though they have always excited suspicion and
criticism. In recent years they have won public approval
for their work in reconstructing and helping war-devastated
lands.

Using the idea of brotherhood as their goal, the Brethren
have stressed Christian living rather than doctrine and
have come to view Jesus more as a lawgiver than as a
Savior. They baptize by immersing the individual three
times and they celebrate the Lord's Supper with a meal
and with footwashing. They will probably never be a
large denomination but they represent a different approach
to the teachings of Christ.

5. *The Salvation Army.* The blaring brass of a Salvation Army band is so well known that it was even fea-
tured in a Broadway musical show (Guys and Dolls) a
few years ago. But the Salvation Army is more than
booming music or the street preaching that follows the

music; it is an interesting combination of evangelism and social work among the downtrodden and neglected.

The organization came into existence through the work of William Booth, a Methodist clergyman who began in 1865 to work among the slum people of London. Most church groups had come to regard these slum dwellers as hopeless, but Booth touched many hearts. His original intention was to supplement the work of the regular churches, but when his converts weren't welcomed he set up his own organization. It was modeled on the British army and had its statement of faith, called Articles of War, its uniforms, an officer's training school, etc.

Booth's belief that a hungry man must be fed before he will hunger for the Word of God is one of the teachings of the Army to this day. However, although it carries on a large program of feeding and caring for those in need, the Salvation Army doesn't overlook evangelism. The Methodist beliefs of the founder are reflected in the group, including an emphasis on complete sanctification or holiness. One glaring omission appears—the sacraments are disregarded completely.

Nevertheless, regardless of doctrinal weaknesses, the fact remains that the Salvation Army has reached many people who were neglected by the regular churches in England and America. The band may be off key at times and the speaker may not be too logical but souls have been saved by the followers of General William Booth.

6. *The Mennonites and Amish.* It is not too uncommon in certain sections of the country to see an old man driving a horse and buggy down a modern highway. The driver will be dressed in plain, somber clothes and will

possess a beard like that of an Old Testament prophet. This man belongs to the Amish, a branch of the Mennonite Church. And in the minds of most people the Mennonites are "queer people" who shun most of the things that seem important in the modern world.

Consider some of their teachings. The Mennonites are pacifists like the Brethren. They believe oaths, capital punishment and wars are a part of the Old Testament dispensation, now replaced by the New. They forbid all kinds of luxury, and for some this includes buttons, telephones, automobiles, razors. They practice footwashing and the giving of a "holy kiss" at communion. The women do not cut their hair and usually wear a small white cap in public.

While the Mennonites differ so much among themselves that one of their own authors says: "There are exceptions to almost anything one can say about them," this wall of separation from contact with the world seems a part of the general pattern.

Actually the Mennonites are one of the oldest Protestant groups, being first organized in Germany by Menno Simons. They came into existence in 1536 during the ferment of the Reformation and represented those who wanted to sweep away everything that the church had built up during the centuries. Plainness and simplicity became their watchword. Christian living was stressed so that even today there are great doctrinal differences in the church, while deviation in Christian living is dealt with by banning the member and even cutting him off from all community life. Despite doctrinal tolerance, there are 21 different groups of Mennonites, with the Amish representing the strictest of the strict.

The modern world is having its effect on these people. It is not easy to remain isolated any more today. Many of the young people turn from the conservative to the more liberal branches of the church, and others drift away. It remains to be seen whether this ancient church of the Reformation can survive in a 20th century world.

7. *The Society of Friends* (Quakers). It's interesting to note how people come to the same conclusions through different routes. The Quakers, like the Mennonites and the Brethren, are opposed to all war, to the taking of oaths and to capital punishment. Yet their reason for such a viewpoint is entirely different. They base their view not on direct statements from the Bible but on the distinctive Quaker doctrine of the Inner Light.

The Society of Friends was started by George Fox during the religious upheaval that came in England under Oliver Cromwell. It was a period when all authority was being questioned. Fox found many willing to accept his teaching that all men had an Inner Light within which would guide them in religious matters. This did not mean that Fox rejected the Bible, but the light within would guide a man into the truth.

Such a view had radical ramifications. It meant that all men were equal since all men had this light. In obedience to this view, Quakers refused to remove their hats in the presence of kings or judges. The Inner Light meant war was wrong since this would mean the killing of someone else who had that Inner Light. Capital punishment was attacked and slavery was criticized on the same basis.

The established church was also under attack, for the Quakers insisted that every man, not only clergy, could testify. Many Quaker churches still have no pastors but simply meet and wait for the Spirit to move someone to speak.

Fox's views quickly provoked persecution. Quakers were cruelly tortured. Many fled to America and were welcomed to the Quaker colony, Pennsylvania. When the persecution ceased some of the zeal went out of the church too. It began to grow more slowly and is a relatively small group today.

Quakers now turn their energy to charitable work, and for a small church they have done remarkable things in relieving the suffering of the world. The doctrine of the Inner Light has made other doctrines rather vague among most Quakers. Some branches of the church have taught orthodox Christianity; others have been virtually Unitarian in their views. The Sacraments have been almost entirely ignored. But the keen social conscience of the Quakers has proven a blessing to other churches.

8. *Covenant Church and Free Church of America.* State churches usually invite opposition, and the Lutheran churches in Scandinavia are no exception. In the great religious revivals that stirred Norway, Sweden and Denmark during the last century, a number of "free" churches and missionary societies were organized outside the state church. When some of the people touched by these revivals came to America, the result was the establishment of similar churches in America.

The Evangelical Covenant Church was once known as the Swedish Evangelical Mission Covenant Church, thus indicating its origin. This church came into existence with the merger of two groups in 1885. While the origin is

Lutheran in a sense, there are no really binding doctrines. The emphasis is on personal salvation, on consecrated living and on the establishment of missions.

The Evangelical Free Church of America came into existence in 1950 through the merger of two free church groups. All three Scandinavian countries were represented in these churches. The new body differs from the Covenant church in that greater liberty is given to the individual churches in doctrinal matters. The only requirement for membership is conversion and the willingness to live the Christian life. Baptism is usually by immersion.

9. *The Old Catholic Churches.* In the year 1870. The Roman Catholic Church declared that when the pope speaks under certain circumstances, he is infallible. This statement was made only after considerable quarreling in the church, and there were some who refused to accept such a viewpoint. Consequently, in Germany, Holland and Switzerland certain groups split away from the Church of Rome and called themselves "Old Catholic Churches."

Almost immediately an effort was made to establish similar churches in America and this was mildly successful. However, because of disagreements and controversies, the Old Catholic Churches in America are no longer affiliated with the European group. The largest domestic church is known as the North American Old Roman Catholic Church.

In general, Old Catholic Churches lean toward the Eastern Orthodox teachings. The Roman Mass with some changes is followed, but the language used by the congregation (rather than Latin) is employed in the service. Priests are permitted to marry. Papal infallibility is denied, but most other teachings associated with the word "Catholic" are retained.

10. *The Moravians.* Every denomination, in order to continue to exist as a separate organization, must possess some distinctive teaching or emphasis. The Moravian Church has three—Unity, Piety, Christian Mission Work. In some ways this is the oldest Protestant church in America, for the Moravians owe their beginnings to John Huss, the Bohemian reformer who was burned at the stake in 1415. Despite severe persecutions, the church of Huss continued to live and found new life in America. Its leader in early Pennsylvania was Count Zinzendorf, a German prince who considered himself a Lutheran all his life.

Caught up by the terrible persecutions and religious hatreds of the 16th and 17th centuries, the Moravians put much stress on Christian unity. They tried to encourage Lutherans and the Reformed to base their fellowship on piety rather than doctrine. The motto of the church has always been: "In essentials, unity; in non-essentials, liberty; in all things, charity." While they haven't succeeded in uniting the churches, the Moravians despite their smallness, have touched the lives of many religious leaders, including John Wesley.

Piety, Christian living, has also been a strong point among the Moravians. Strangely, this hasn't been achieved by preaching the law, for the emphasis has been on the love of God shown in the redemptive life of Christ. Sometimes the piety has been a little sentimental but Christian living has blossomed among the Moravians.

It's hard to realize that there was a time when Protestant churches weren't interested in mission work. Yet such was the case. The Moravians began the first mission work and have continued to be a missionary church. They have sent workers far out of proportion to their numbers. Today they still conduct mission stations in 13 fields.

While there are no important doctrinal emphases, the church does practice infant baptism and confirmation. The Moravians have been considerably enriched by their music and liturgy and by their stress on a trained clergy.

Conclusion. This survey of your neighbor's faith has been long and complicated. There have been things to praise and things to criticize. As we look at ourselves and those around us, we can't help feeling sorry that the Church has been so tragically divided. We can't help seeing also that God has kept His Church alive in many places, despite our divisions and shortcomings. And we should be moved to pray, to pray for forgiveness of our errors and for a new and greater demonstration of unity in the future.

About the Author

William A. Poovey is associate professor of homiletics at Wartburg Theological Seminary, Dubuque, Iowa, and author of several books and plays.

A native of Baltimore, Md., he has degrees from Capital University and Seminary, Columbus, Ohio, and Northwestern University, Evanston, Ill. He also has studied at Union Theological Seminary.

Mr. Poovey held pastorates at Monterey Park, Calif., San Antonio, Texas, and Memphis, Tenn., before assuming his present teaching post.

Books he has written include *Questions That Trouble Christians*, *Problems That Plague the Saints* and *No Hands But Ours*. He was a co-author of *Hymn Dramatizations* and author of the Sunday School Lesson appearing in the Lutheran Standard from 1956 to 1960.

Mr. Poovey is a member of the commission for research and social action, The American Lutheran Church, and a past member of the board of Christian social action, American Lutheran Church.